Physical Education Pedagogies for Health

This book focusses on health within physical education (PE) and specifically on PE pedagogies for health. It gives practitioners and students the knowledge, understanding, skills and confidence to employ effective health pedagogies and practices in their work, and to promote healthy, active lifestyles within their PE curricula.

Drawing on cutting-edge research, the book highlights key pedagogical issues and debates concerning the delivery of health in PE, and their implications for practice, such as in policy and curriculum development. It explores recent recommendations and developments in PE pedagogies for health which have been shown to enhance, or have the potential to enhance, practice in the area, as well as future opportunities for doing so. It provides practical tools that bridge the gap between research and application, including learning activities and questions that encourage the reader to reflect on their own professional practice and identify actions for developing their own pedagogy, practice and curricula in the area.

This is essential reading for all PE teachers, coaches working with children or young people, teacher and coach educators, and trainee teachers and coaches.

Lorraine Cale is a Professor in Physical Education and Sport Pedagogy and the Director of Teacher Education at Loughborough University, UK, as well as Adjunct Professor at the University of Limerick, Ireland. Lorraine's research centres on the promotion of physical activity and healthy lifestyles within schools, both within and beyond the curriculum.

Jo Harris is an Emeritus Professor of Physical Education and Sport Pedagogy, and former Director of Teacher Education at Loughborough University, UK. Jo's research focusses on health-related learning in physical education and the promotion of active lifestyles.

Routledge Focus on Sport Pedagogy
Series editor: Ash Casey, Loughborough University, UK

The field of sport pedagogy (physical education and coaching) is united by the desire to improve the experiences of young people and adult participants. The *Routledge Focus on Sport Pedagogy* series presents small books on big topics in an effort to eradicate the boundaries that currently exist between young people, adult learners, coaches, teachers and academics, in schools, clubs and universities. Theoretically grounded but with a strong emphasis on practice, the series aims to open up important and useful new perspectives on teaching, coaching and learning in sport and physical education.

Meaningful Physical Education
An Approach for Teaching and Learning
Edited by Tim Fletcher, Déirdre Ní Chróinín, Douglas Gleddie and Stephanie Beni

Pedagogies of Social Justice in Physical Education and Youth Sport
Shrehan Lynch, Jennifer L. Walton-Fisette and Carla Luguetti

Learner-Oriented Teaching and Assessment in Youth Sport
Edited by Cláudio Farias and Isabel Mesquita

Physical Education Pedagogies for Health
Edited by Lorraine Cale and Jo Harris

For more information about this series, please visit: https://www.routledge.com/Routledge-Focus-on-Sport-Pedagogy/book-series/RFSPED

Physical Education Pedagogies for Health

**Edited by
Lorraine Cale and Jo Harris**

Routledge
Taylor & Francis Group

LONDON AND NEW YORK

First published 2023
by Routledge
4 Park Square, Milton Park, Abingdon, Oxon OX14 4RN

and by Routledge
605 Third Avenue, New York, NY 10158

Routledge is an imprint of the Taylor & Francis Group, an informa business

British Library Cataloguing-in-Publication Data
A catalogue record for this book is available from the British Library

Library of Congress Cataloging-in-Publication Data
Names: Cale, Lorraine, editor. | Harris, Jo, 1955- editor.
Title: Physical education pedagogies for health / Lorraine Cale, Jo
Harris.
Description: New York : Routledge, 2022. |
Series: Routledge Focus on Sport Pedagogy | Includes
bibliographical references and index. |
Identifiers: LCCN 2022015053 | ISBN 9781032127163 (Hardback) |
ISBN 9781032127170 (Paperback) | ISBN 9781003225904 (eBook)
Subjects: LCSH: Physical education and training. | Health
education—Study and teaching (Elementary) | Physical education
for children—Curricula.
Classification: LCC GV341 .P475 2022 | DDC 796.071—dc23/
eng/20220517
LC record available at https://lccn.loc.gov/2022015053

ISBN: 978-1-032-12716-3 (hbk)
ISBN: 978-1-032-12717-0 (pbk)
ISBN: 978-1-003-22590-4 (ebk)

DOI: 10.4324/9781003225904

Typeset in Times New Roman
by codeMantra

We, Lorraine and Jo, would like to dedicate this book to Dr Len Almond who supervised our PhDs, inspired us greatly, and whose influence still drives us to want to make advancements to health-based PE today.

Contents

Figures

Tables

Contributors

Laura Alfrey is a Course Leader for the Bachelor of Education (Health and Physical Education) at Monash University, Australia. Her research focusses on health and physical education, sport and physical activity contexts, and the ways in which policy, professional learning and practice contribute to inclusive and educative experiences for young people.

Kathleen Armour is the Vice-Provost (Education and Student Experience) at the University of Central London, UK. Prior to this, she was Pro-Vice Chancellor (Education) at the University of Birmingham, UK. Kathleen's research is in education and in career-long professional learning, and she is particularly interested in bridging the gaps between theory/research and practice.

Mark Bowler is a Principal Lecturer and Portfolio Leader for Undergraduate provision in the School of Teacher Education at the University of Bedfordshire, UK. His research includes approaches to promoting healthy, active lifestyles in young people and to designing and teaching the physical education curriculum.

Nicola Carse is Deputy Head of the Institute of Sport, Physical Education and Health Sciences in the Moray House School of Education and Sport at the University of Edinburgh, UK. Her main areas of research include primary physical education, teacher professional learning, curriculum development, complexity thinking, self-study and practitioner enquiry.

Ash Casey is a Reader in Physical Education Pedagogy and the Programme Leader for Physical Education Teacher Education at Loughborough University, UK and Series Editor of the Routledge Focus on Sport Pedagogy series. His research focusses on

Models-Based Practice, teacher learning/research and the use of new technologies in learning.

Victoria Goodyear is a Senior Lecturer in Pedagogy of Sport, Physical Activity and Health at the University of Birmingham, UK. Her research focusses on understanding and enhancing young people's health and well-being through research on pedagogy and digital technologies, areas in which she has given numerous international talks and keynote presentations as well as communicated her research to policy and the media.

Mike Jess is a Senior Lecturer at the University of Edinburgh, UK. His main research interest focusses on the relationship between complexity-related perspectives and educational practice in physical education. Recently, this work has concentrated on self-study, teacher vision, lesson study, complex leadership, transdisciplinarity and boundary crossing.

Dillon Landi is a Lecturer in Education at the University of Strathclyde, UK and is a former teacher and subject supervisor. He teaches in the areas of sociology of education, health and well-being, gender and sexuality, and qualitative research methods.

Paul McMillan is a Lecturer in Physical Education in the Moray House School of Education and Sport at the University of Edinburgh, UK. His main research interests include pedagogy, teacher vision, lesson study and self-study which he draws on to inform his undergraduate and postgraduate teaching and work with teachers in schools.

Paul Sammon is a Senior Lecturer and Teacher Educator in Physical Education at the University of Bedfordshire, UK and also coordinates a professional learning programme for primary teachers. His research interests include promoting active lifestyles, Models-Based Practice and teacher professional learning.

Acknowledgements

We also wish to acknowledge all the colleagues, teachers and trainees we have worked with over the years who have supported, implemented and provided feedback to us on our work, and motivated us to want to continue to develop and improve pedagogy and practice in this area.

1 The Role of Physical Education in Health

Expectations, Challenges and Opportunities

Jo Harris and Lorraine Cale

Introduction

This chapter sets the context for the remainder of the book. It considers the growing expectation on schools and PE to take on health outcomes and reflects on the opportunities as well as challenges to effectively achieving these. Specifically, the chapter explores why PE is seen to have a role and responsibility in health, and considers what it can realistically strive to achieve in this respect. It also suggests future opportunities and possibilities for PE teachers to contribute to public health by supporting students in leading active lifestyles. This is needed now more than ever, given that, for most children around the world, physical activity levels reduced during the recent global pandemic (Rossi, Behme & Breuer, 2021).

The chapter initially discusses the role and responsibilities of PE in relation to health. It then outlines policy and curricular expectations in this area and some challenges to meeting these. PE teachers are encouraged to reflect on the extent to which their current PE curriculum meets health-related expectations and supports their students in adopting an active way of life. They are also asked to consider ways of addressing some of the challenges to meeting health-related expectations and maximising the opportunities available to them in this endeavour.

After reading this chapter, you will be able to:

i engage in key debates associated with the role and responsibilities of PE in relation to health;
ii understand health-related policy and curricular expectations;
iii identify and critique challenges to meeting health-related expectations;
iv address health-related challenges and maximise opportunities to promote health.

DOI: 10.4324/9781003225904-1

The Role and Responsibilities of PE in Relation to Health

It is widely advocated that schools can and should play a major role in contributing to public health, given their skilled workforce and ability to reach and influence virtually all children and their families (World Health Organisation [WHO], 2018). Interest in this role has heightened in recent decades due to growing concerns about young people's health. For example, depression has become a leading cause of ill health among adolescents; furthermore, half of all mental health disorders start by age 14 but most remain undetected and extend into adulthood, impairing both physical and mental health and limiting opportunities to lead fulfilling lives (WHO, 2021). An additional escalating health concern relates to the prevalence of overweight or obese children and adolescents, which increased more than fourfold between 1975 and 2016 from 4% to 18% globally (WHO, 2016).

To help address concerns about young people's health, schools around the world have been encouraged to adopt whole-school approaches to health promotion and the pursuit of health enhancing behaviours, such as being routinely active (WHO, 2018). With respect to the latter, physical activity levels among young people are decreasing, with global estimates indicating that 81% of adolescents do not meet the WHO recommendations for physical activity. There are also notable inequalities with girls being less active than boys in most countries and significant differences between higher and lower economic groups and between countries and regions (WHO, 2020).

Low levels of physical activity among young people are concerning, especially given increasing evidence that being regularly active during childhood provides physical, mental and social health benefits (Biddle & Asare, 2011; Janssen & LeBlanc, 2010). This evidence provides a strong rationale for the need to promote healthy, active lifestyles and has led to attention being paid to the potential role schools and in particular PE can play in this regard.

PE's relationship with health is long-standing and generally accepted, given that it provides young people with regular opportunities to engage in physical activity and learn about the health gains associated with an active way of life. PE's contribution to public health is mostly perceived positively (Harris & Cale, 2019) and indeed, health has increasingly become the leading justification for the subject in schools (Kirk, 2018). Consequently, PE is expected to play a vital role in, and share responsibility for, enhancing health, and the promotion of active lifestyles has become an established goal of PE curricula globally (e.g. Australian Curriculum, Assessment and Reporting Authority (ACARA), 2012; Department for Education (DfE), 2013; New Zealand Ministry of Education (NZMoE), 2020).

In this respect, it is advocated that PE's role and responsibility should be to stimulate interest, enjoyment, knowledge, competence and expertise in physical activity and sport for health and well-being (Fox, Cooper & McKenna, 2004) among all young people. This includes equipping them with the knowledge and skills to access and appraise resources and evaluate personal progress towards active living (Macdonald, Enright & McCuaig 2018), and to critique health information and messages from sources beyond school, so that they feel empowered and can make informed, independent decisions about their health and physical activity behaviours (Cale, 2021). In summary, young people need to be supported to become lifelong, critical consumers of health-related information and possess the skills to access, appraise and apply health-related knowledge.

Box 1.1 PE's Role and Responsibilities in Relation to Health

Reflect on PE's role and responsibilities in relation to health by considering the following questions:

1   How important is PE's role in promoting health? How do you see this role playing out in practice?
2   What level of responsibility should PE have for promoting active lifestyles? With whom should this responsibility be shared?

Health-Related Policy and Curricular Expectations

Within the context just described, PE is viewed to be particularly suited to advocating and leading on a whole-school approach to promoting active lifestyles. In England, for example, health education is a compulsory subject in the National Curriculum, which incorporates teaching students about the characteristics and benefits of an active way of life and the risks associated with a sedentary lifestyle (DfE, 2019). In addition, a specific aim of the PE curriculum in England is that all students lead healthy, active lives (DfE, 2013). To help meet this aim, primary school-aged children are expected to become increasingly competent and confident movers via accessing a broad range of opportunities, and secondary school aged children are expected to develop interest and confidence in a range of activities outside of school and in later life, understand and pursue the long-term benefits of physical activity, develop personal fitness and pursue active, healthy lives (DfE, 2013).

There are similar health-related expectations in PE in other UK countries. In addition, reforms in the PE curricula in Australia and New Zealand have resulted in increased health-related expectations. For example, the Australian Health and Physical Education curriculum incorporates the development of health literacy skills and adopts a critical enquiry-based approach (ACARA, 2012). Likewise, the PE curriculum in New Zealand has shifted towards a concern for well-being and has underlying concepts which guide learning such as Hauora (a Maori philosophy of well-being), health promotion and a socio-ecological perspective (NZMoE, 2020).

The above demonstrates that, although national PE curricula vary across the world, health is a prominent theme and the aim of promoting healthy, active lifestyles is well established. Chapter 2 explores how this is expressed and can be achieved within PE.

Box 1.2 Health-Related Expectations

Consider the following questions relating to health-related expectations of schools and PE:

1 Are the health-related expectations of schools and PE realistic?
2 In what ways does your school and PE curriculum support students in leading active lifestyles? How effective is this?

Challenges to Meeting Health-Related Expectations

Despite the widespread recognition that schools play a major role in contributing to public health, there are a number of challenges to effectively fulfilling this role. A key challenge is that behaviour change is complex, and schools have little or no influence on important factors affecting young people's health such as genetics, the environment and family modelling. Moreover, the core business of schools is focussed on educational outcomes and there is inevitable tension in schools additionally taking on public health outcomes, especially given their limited capacity, funding and time (Gard & Pluim, 2014).

Furthermore, and with respect to PE, there continue to be long-standing debates about the purpose of the subject and how this is expressed in practice. PE has multiple objectives and health promotion is just one of these alongside others such as the development of physical competence, social skills and moral values (Lounsbery et al., 2011). Indeed, the appropriateness of a public health goal for the subject has been questioned by some (e.g. Evans, Rich & Davies, 2004; Kirk, 2018), and there is uncertainty about the 'proper role for PE in health' and the level of responsibility the profession should accept for children's health outcomes (Armour & Harris, 2013, p. 209). Some physical educators recognise and welcome the potential of the subject to achieve health outcomes but are mindful of significant constraints to realistically achieving this potential (Fox, Cooper & McKenna, 2004). These constraints include addressing the multiple and often competing objectives within limited curriculum time (Fardy, Azzollini & Herman, 2004). As discussed by Cale (2021) in her outline of PE's journey on the road to health, the subject cannot meet all of young people's physical activity and health needs, be held responsible for improving young people's health, nor can it solve societal health problems such as obesity and physical inactivity.

In addition, PE curricula that are overly focussed on objectives such as skill development have been criticised for not offering activities considered to be more effective in promoting regular physical activity (Trost, 2004). Further concerns have been reported about the way in which health is expressed and taught in PE, which has been found to be inconsistent and somewhat 'hit and miss' (Harris & Cale, 2019). Research also suggests that the learning associated with health can be minimal and narrow, and based on a limited and limiting discourse of health (Evans et al., 2008) which prioritises physical health over mental and social health and tends to be simplistic and reductive in nature (Hooper, Harris & Cale, 2022). Alongside this, are concerns about potentially detrimental health-related practices in PE such as dreary drill and monotonous cross-country, and the dominance of fitness testing and training regimes (Cale & Harris, 2009; Evans et al., 2008). Chapter 3 provides more detailed consideration of fitness testing as a debated and contested PE-for-health practice. Suffice to say here is that this, and other such practices, suggest a lack of alignment between PE teachers' health-related philosophies and their practices with many declaring an intent to promote healthy, active lifestyles yet trying to achieve this through a narrow and potentially off-putting range of fitness testing and training activities (Harris & Leggett, 2015).

A further challenge is the somewhat vulnerable position of PE within a neoliberal context in which privatised reforms such as increased marketisation and performativity adversely affect the potentialities of PE (Evans & Davies, 2015; Macdonald, 2011). These debilitating influences seem most prominent in the area of health-related PE. For example, the dominance of fitness testing and regular calls for national fitness testing reflect the emphasis on high stakes testing within a broader neoliberal policy climate (Macdonald, 2011). This is despite counter-arguments that fitness testing in PE may well represent a misdirected effort in the promotion of active lifestyles (Cale & Harris, 2009). The pervasiveness of neoliberal agendas has also led to concerns about health promotion outcomes being unattainable for the profession, the narrowing of PE to what can be measured and an overemphasis on individual children's body shape or weight or fitness such that again, PE becomes a negative experience (Cale & Harris, 2009; Tinning, 2000). Furthermore, increased marketisation has led to a range of providers (e.g. health, fitness and exercise instructors) and products (e.g. those focussing on fitness scores, body weight measures and training plans), which claim to address public health crises such as low activity and fitness levels and increased obesity among young people (Evans, 2014). This further reinforces a narrow and limiting approach to health plus implies that there are simple, quick fixes to long-standing, complex societal health issues.

The concerns identified above are heightened by issues associated with the availability and uptake of initial and continuing professional development (CPD) for teachers relating to whole-school and subject-specific approaches to health promotion. Indeed, there has been limited attention to this area of CPD, and particularly to the development of PE-for-health pedagogies (Cale, Harris & Duncombe, 2016) which could provide clarity about how best to achieve health-enhancing PE. In terms of limitations in initial teacher education, Harris (2014) revealed inadequacies in the preparation of trainee PE teachers to promote active lifestyles and called for radical changes to PE teacher education, especially the school-based provision. There is also the identified 'conundrum' of many PE teachers having misguided confidence in their ability to teach health-related PE and consequently choosing not to pursue professional development in this area even when it is available (Alfrey, Cale & Webb, 2012). Collectively, the above have resulted in calls for a critical approach to helping students to achieve healthy, active lifestyles in the form of new, evidence-based PE-for-health pedagogies (Armour & Harris, 2013; Kirk, 2006). Chapters 4–6 introduce and discuss examples of PE-for-health pedagogies, approaches and models.

Box 1.3 Challenges to Meeting Health-Related Expectations

Reflect on the challenges to meeting health-related expectations by considering the following questions:

1   Which, if any, of these challenges have you encountered in your school? Have you come across any additional barriers?
2   As applicable, in what ways have these challenges/barriers affected your practice? Have you been able to address or overcome any of these? If so, in what ways?

Addressing Health-Related Challenges and Maximising Opportunities to Promote Health within and through PE

There are now a growing number of government agendas and initiatives which prioritise health promotion and which can support schools and teachers in addressing some of the health-related challenges just identified. For example, in England, there are national health-enhancing social media campaigns entitled 'Better Health' and 'Change4Life' (National Health Service, 2021a, 2021b) to which teachers can make important connections. Another national social media campaign in England, 'This Girl Can', has a physical activity focus and aims to enhance the self-esteem and confidence of girls and women to move, regardless of their shape, size and ability (Sport England, 2021a). Health-related challenges can also be addressed through engagement in health-related work involving national PE and sport organisations such as the Association for Physical Education (afPE) and the Youth Sport Trust (YST) in the UK and the Australian Council for Health, Physical Education and Recreation. A specific example in England is a Sport England (2021b) initiative working in partnership with afPE, the YST, the Activity Alliance and the Teaching Schools Council. This focusses on the promotion of active lifestyles in secondary schools and involves upskilling teachers to improve the quality and breadth of PE provision, so that it acts as a catalyst for achieving outcomes such as improved mental well-being, resilience and confidence.

Alongside making explicit links to national health-promoting campaigns and initiatives, PE teachers can address health-related challenges by making selective and effective use of technological advancements (which is the focus of Chapter 7), and by being an advocate for a whole-school approach to maximise opportunities to promote healthy behaviours among students (see Chapter 4). In this respect, cross-curricular links are encouraged, which help to connect health-related learning (e.g. about the effects of exercise or the risks of a sedentary lifestyle) across subjects such as PE, Science, and Personal, Social and Health Education, thereby improving the coherence and effectiveness of students' health-related learning (see Chapter 2). Incorporating activity breaks during the school day has also been found to improve concentration and behaviour (Donnelly & Lambourne, 2011) as well as increase physical activity (Lowden et al., 2001). Schools can furthermore encourage the adoption of active pedagogies across all subjects which involve students moving as part of the learning experience (Harris & Cale, 2019). This approach equally extends to and has value in PE as research has shown activity levels during PE lessons to be surprisingly low (Fairclough & Stratton, 2006; Hobbs et al., 2015).

Finally, recent studies have focussed on addressing known health-related challenges in PE through a variety of pedagogical approaches and this has become a developing area of research with some encouraging outcomes reported to date. For example, in the US, Weaver et al. (2018) involved PE teachers in a participatory-based, competency building professional workshop focussed on implementing physical activity promoting practices (e.g. using small-sided games, reducing queues, avoiding elimination activities), finding these to have a positive influence on students' physical activity within PE. In addition, Bowler (2019) and Sammon (2019) in the UK explored the development and application of a health-based PE model, which forefronts 'valuing a physically active life' as its primary goal and found that collaborative and sustained professional development supported teachers to adopt new ideas and change their practices over time. These and other studies have attempted to address the challenges that PE teachers face when teaching PE for health, including gaps in their knowledge and understanding and narrow and limiting curriculum discourses around health. Chapters 4 and 5 provide more details about the health-based PE model, while Chapter 6 focusses on another study and pedagogical approach known as the Promoting Active Lifestyles (PAL) Project.

Box 1.4 Final Reflections

Reflect on the meaning and consider the implications of the following quotations, which relate to ongoing health-related issues:

- 'If "exercise is medicine", physical education is the pill not taken' (McKenzie & Lounsbery, 2009, p. 219).
- 'Reducing 'health' to only the most obvious aspects of measured performance (e.g. weight, height, exercise levels) while promoting the message at all ages and stages of schooling that healthy equals thin, should carry a government health warning' (Evans, 2007).
- '… it may be better for physical educators to say nothing about obesity, exercise and health, rather than singing the praises of slimness and vigorous exercise and condemning the evils of fat and 'sedentary life' (Gard & Wright, 2001, p. 535).

Conclusion

This chapter has focussed on the role of PE in relation to health and revealed that the partnership between education and health is neither smooth nor straightforward. Indeed, caution has been expressed about what schools and PE can realistically achieve in terms of health outcomes, and there are concerns about some practices in PE which have been implemented in the name of health. So, while health-related expectations of PE are high and somewhat aspirational, the challenges to meeting these are complicated and numerous. This is not to say that schools and PE should not strive to make significant contributions to public health nor that they cannot positively influence the lifestyles of their students. Rather, these endeavours should be passionately and persistently pursued with full awareness and acknowledgement of the complexity of behaviour change among young people, and full understanding of the challenges to meeting health-related expectations within school settings. This will help to ensure that future health-related possibilities in PE are evidence-based, more sophisticated and sustainable.

Summary and Recommendations

- Schools and PE are expected to play a major role in health and this responsibility has heightened due to escalating concerns about young people's health. Young people's physical activity levels are low, which has led to an increasing expectation that PE specifically should play a leading role in promoting active lifestyles.
- Schools are encouraged to adopt whole-school approaches to health promotion, and the promotion of healthy, active lifestyles has become a prominent theme in PE-specific curricula globally.
- Challenges to PE teachers effectively contributing to public health include them having little or no influence on key factors affecting young people's health, and limited time, capacity and resources to pursue both education and health outcomes.
- There is uncertainty about the level of responsibility PE should accept for children's health outcomes and concerns about the expression of health in PE, associated with a lack of alignment between PE teachers' health-related philosophies and practices. Neoliberal agendas have also led to debilitating influences on health-related PE such as an overemphasis on fitness testing and on body weight. However, despite the uncertainty and concerns, PE clearly has a role to play in health promotion and can and should be contributing to public health.
- There has been limited attention to health in teachers' initial and continuing professional development and many PE teachers have misguided confidence in their ability to teach health-related PE. This has led to calls for evidence-based PE-for-health pedagogies.
- Within a whole-school approach, PE teachers are well placed to lead or support school-wide initiatives. They should also encourage and facilitate cross-curricular links to improve the effectiveness of health-related learning across subjects and activity breaks to increase students' physical activity, concentration and behaviour.
- Schools can adopt active pedagogies that require students to move as part of the learning experience. They can also pursue research-informed pedagogical approaches to promoting health within PE

which have been found to enhance students' health-related learning and physical activity.

- We recommend that, during this current academic year, teachers review their PE curriculum in terms of how well it supports and drives school-wide efforts to promote healthy, active lifestyles and meets subject-specific health-related expectations.
- In preparation for the next academic year, we recommend that teachers connect with national health-promoting campaigns and initiatives and consider adopting research-informed pedagogical approaches to promoting health within PE.

References

Alfrey, L., Cale, L., & Webb, L. (2012). Physical education teachers' continuing professional development in health-related exercise. *Physical Education and Sport Pedagogy*, 17(5), 477–491.

Armour, K., & Harris, J. (2013). Making the case for developing new PE-for-health pedagogies. *Quest*, *65*(2), 201–219.

Australian Curriculum, Assessment and Reporting Authority. (2012). *Australian Curriculum. Health and Physical Education.* Sydney: Australian Curriculum, Assessment and Reporting Authority.

Biddle, S., & Asare, M. (2011). Physical activity and mental health in children and adolescents: A review of reviews. *British Journal of Sports Medicine*, 45(11), 886–895.

Bowler, M.T. (2019). *Developing a Pedagogical Model for Health-based Physical Education.* A Doctoral Thesis. Loughborough University. https://hdl.handle.net/2134/37704.

Cale, L. (2021). Physical education's journey on the road to health. *Sport, Education and Society*, 26(5), 486–499.

Cale, L., & Harris, J. (2009). Fitness testing in physical education – A misdirected effort in promoting healthy lifestyles and physical activity? *Physical Education and Sport Pedagogy*, 14(1), 89–108.

Cale, L., Harris, J., & Duncombe, R. (2016). Promoting physical activity in secondary schools: Growing expectations, same 'old' issues? *European Physical Education Review*, 22(4), 526–544.

Department for Education. (2013). *National Curriculum in England: Physical Education Programmes of Study.* London: Department for Education.

Department for Education. (2019). *Healthy Schools Rating Scheme. Guidance for Schools.* London: Department for Education.

Donnelly, J.E., & Lambourne, K. (2011). Classroom-based physical activity, cognition, and academic achievement. *Preventive Medicine*, 52, S36–S42.

Evans, J. (2007). Health education or weight management in schools? *Cardiometabolic Risk and Weight Management*, 2(2), 12–16.

Evans, J. (2014). Neoliberalism and the future for a socio-educative physical education. *Physical Education and Sport Pedagogy*, 19(5), 545–558.

Evans, J., & Davies, B. (2015). Neoliberal freedoms, privatisation and the future of physical education. *Sport, Education and Society*, 20(1), 10–26.

Evans, J., Rich, E., & Davies, B. (2004). The emperor's new clothes: Fat, thin and overweight. The social fabrication of risk and ill health. *Journal of Teaching in Physical Education*, 23(4), 372–391.

Evans, J., Rich, E., Davies, B., & Allwood, R. (2008). *Education, Disordered Eating and Obesity Discourse. Fat Fabrications*. Oxon: Routledge.

Fairclough, S., & Stratton, G. (2006). A review of physical activity levels during elementary school physical education. *Journal of Teaching Physical Education*, 25, 240–258.

Fardy, P.S., Azzollini, A., & Herman, A. (2004). Developing public health-based physical education in urban schools. *Journal of Teaching in Physical Education*, 23, 359–371.

Fox, K.R., Cooper, A., & McKenna, J. (2004). The school and promotion of children's health-enhancing physical activity: Perspectives from the United Kingdom. *Journal of Teaching in Physical Education*, 23(4), 338–358.

Gard, M., & Pluim, C. (2014). *Schools and Public Health: Past, Present, Future*. Plymouth: Lexington Books.

Gard, M., & Wright, J. (2001). Managing uncertainty: Obesity discourses and physical education in a risk society. *Studies in Philosophy and Education*, 20(6), 535–549.

Harris, J. (2014). Physical education teacher education students' knowledge, perceptions and experiences of promoting healthy, active lifestyles in secondary schools. *Physical Education and Sport Pedagogy*, 19(5), 466–480.

Harris, J., & Cale, L. (2019). *Promoting Active Lifestyles in Schools*. Champaign, IL: Human Kinetics.

Harris, J., & Leggett, G. (2015). Testing, training and tensions: The expression of health within physical education curricula in secondary schools in England and Wales. *Sport, Education and Society*, 20(3–4), 423–441.

Hobbs, M., Daly-Smith, A., Morley, D., & McKenna, J. (2015). A case study objectively assessing female physical activity levels within the National Curriculum for Physical Education. *European Physical Education Review*, 21(2), 149–161.

Hooper, O., Harris, J., & Cale, L. (2022). Health-related learning in physical education in England. In: J. Stirrup and O. Hooper (Eds.), *Critical Pedagogies in Physical Education, Physical Activity and Health* (pp. 88–102). Oxon: Routledge.

Janssen, I., & LeBlanc, A.G. (2010). Systematic review of the health benefits of physical activity and fitness in school-aged children and youth. *International Journal of Behavioral Nutrition and Physical Activity*, 7(1), 1–16.

Kirk, D. (2006). The obesity 'crisis' and school physical education. *Sport, Education and Society*, 11(2), 121–133.

Kirk, D. (2018). Physical education-as-health promotion: Recent developments and future issues. *Education and Health*, 36(3), 70–75.

Lounsbery, M.A.F., McKenzie, T.L., Trost, S., & Smith, N.J. (2011). Facilitators and barriers to adopting evidence-based physical education in primary schools. *Journal of Physical Activity and Health*, 8(Suppl 1), S17–S25.

Lowden, K., Powney, J., Davidson, J., & James, C. (2001). *The Class Moves! Pilot in Scotland and Wales*. SCRE Centre, University of Glasgow.

Macdonald, D. (2011). Like a fish in water: Physical education policy and practice in the era of neoliberal globalization. *Quest*, 63(1), 36–45.

Macdonald, D., Enright, E., & McCuaig, L. (2018). Re-visioning the Australian curriculum for health and physical education. In: H.A. Lawson (Ed.), *Redesigning Physical Education. An Equity Agenda in which Every Child Matters* (pp. 196–209). Oxon: Routledge.

McKenzie, T.L., & Lounsbery, M.A.F. (2009). School physical education: The pill not taken. *American Journal of Lifestyle Medicine*, 3(3), 219–225.

National Health Service. (2021a). *Better Health*. Accessed 15/10/21 at https://www.nhs.uk/better-health

National Health Service. (2021b). *Change4Life*. Accessed 15/10/21 at https://www.nhs.uk/change4life

New Zealand Ministry of Education. (2020). *Health and Physical Education: Physical Education*. New Zealand Government.

Rossi, L., Behme, N., & Breuer, C. (2021). Physical activity of children and adolescents during the COVID-19 pandemic – A scoping review. *International Journal of Environmental Research and Public Health*, 18(2), 11440.

Sammon, P. (2019). *Adopting a New Model for Health-based Physical Education: The Impact of a Professional Development Programme on Teachers' Pedagogical Practice*. A Doctoral Thesis. Loughborough University. https://doi.org/10.26174/thesis.lboro.8299686

Sport England. (2021a). *This Girl Can*. Accessed 15/10/21 at https://www.thisgirlcan.co.uk

Sport England. (2021b). *Secondary Teacher Training Programme*. Accessed 15/10/21 at https://www.sportengland.org/how-we-can-help/secondary-teacher-training-programme

Tinning, R. (2000). Seeking a realistic contribution: Considering physical education within HPE in New Zealand and Australia. *Journal of Physical Education New Zealand*, 33(3), 8–21.

Trost, S.G. (2004). School physical education in the post-report era: An analysis from public health. *Journal of Teaching in Physical Education*, 23(4), 318–337.

Weaver, R.G., Webster, C.A., Beets, M.W., Brazendale, K., Chandler, J., Schisler, L., & Aziz, M. (2018). Initial outcomes of a participatory-based, competency-building approach to increasing physical education teachers' physical activity promotion and students' physical activity: A pilot study. *Health Education & Behavior*, 45(3), 359–370.

World Health Organisation. (2016). *Report on the Commission on Ending Childhood Obesity.* Geneva, Switzerland: World Health Organisation.

World Health Organisation. (2018). *Global Standards for Health Promoting Schools.* Geneva, Switzerland: World Health Organisation.

World Health Organisation. (2020). *WHO Guidelines on Physical Activity and Sedentary Behaviour.* Geneva, Switzerland: World Health Organisation.

World Health Organisation. (2021). *Adolescent and Young Adult Health.* Geneva, Switzerland: World Health Organisation.

2 Key Health-Related Approaches, Pedagogical Principles and Learning in Physical Education

Lorraine Cale and Jo Harris

Introduction

While contributing to active lifestyles is widely accepted to be a key goal of PE and is a prominent feature of the PE curricula in many countries (see Chapter 1), some of the fundamental considerations and principles which should underpin effective teaching and pedagogy in the area are not always well known or understood. These include, for example, aspects relating to the desired philosophy, content and outcomes of health in PE as well as its organisation within the curriculum. This chapter therefore focusses on some of these fundamentals. First, it outlines some of the key pedagogical principles and the learning which should underpin the teaching of health in PE. Then the different organisational approaches to health within PE, the relative merits and drawbacks of each, and the factors to take into account when making decisions about the organisation of health in PE are explored. Throughout, teachers are encouraged to reflect on the teaching and learning and organisation of this within their own PE curricula.

After reading this chapter, you will be able to:

i identify the fundamental considerations and pedagogical principles deemed to underpin the effective teaching of health in PE;
ii identify the breadth and scope of health-related learning in PE;
iii explain and critique the different organisational approach(es) to health in PE;
iv reflect on your own and/or your department's philosophy and teaching of health in PE in light of the above.

DOI: 10.4324/9781003225904-2

Philosophy and Content Underpinning Health in PE

It has been claimed that for the teaching of health in PE to be effective it may need a different pedagogical and philosophical approach and emphasis and a new or alternative knowledge base (Armour & Harris, 2013). Historically, and arguably still today, a strong performance-oriented philosophy has dominated PE, with traditional activities such as competitive sport, skills and techniques characterising the subject (Alfrey, Cale & Webb, 2012; Kirk, 2010). In other words, the standard pedagogical approach has been activity focussed where the curriculum/activities are identified first. To the contrary, it is argued that PE-for-health pedagogies should take the learner as the starting point and put their needs at the core (Armour & Harris, 2013). In this regard, Armour and Harris (2013) also advocated the importance of flexible and person-alised pedagogies to accommodate the needs and interests of all students. This reinforces the philosophy and the associated messages which stemmed from a seminal article on health in PE in the early 1990s entitled 'Learning to Care' (Harris & Almond, 1991) which called for a shift away from an activity focussed curriculum and a preoccupation with sport and traditional activities towards a focus on the 'child'. Harris and Almond (1991, p. 6) highlighted how the notion of 'every child' and the belief that 'everyone can be good at physical activity' and 'everyone has the right to positive physical activity experiences' are central to health in PE. Related philosophical principles and messages underpinning health in PE which stemmed from early work in the area include that:

- physical activity is for all
- physical activity is for life
- everyone can be good at physical activity
- everyone can benefit from physical activity
- everyone can find the right kind of physical activity for them
- excellence in physical activity is maintaining an active way of life

(see Harris & Cale, 2019)

In short, these principles and messages advocate an explicit commitment to inclusion, equity, democracy, empowerment and a refocussing towards physical activity for life. These are clearly positive messages to share with students and to support them to realise through positive pedagogical practice.

In order to support teachers in creating and achieving the above, a number of enabling practices and equally some inhibiting ones have been identified with the intention that teachers strive to adopt the former and avoid the latter. These practices are summarised in Table 2.1. It is hoped that by adopting a learner-centred philosophy and approach and paying attention to these, PE teachers can help all young people to learn to love being active, and through this and the pursuit of an active lifestyle, enable them to 'flourish' (Cale, 2021, p. 489).

With regards empowering young people within health in PE, Elbourn and James (2013) identified content, context and pedagogy to be important elements with the former involving a range of physical activities which are safe, progressive, relevant, well informed, inclusive and fun. These might include the following activities and contexts: sport (lifestyle sports, play sport and competitive sport), dance, outdoor adventure, fitness-related activities (e.g. aerobics and circuit training) as well as other health-related aspects of learning such as lifestyle management and goal setting (Cale, 2021). Health-related learning and different approaches to the organisation of this learning are considered in the following sections.

A further important principle to the teaching of health in PE is that learning should be experiential and involve the acquisition of a

Table 2.1 Enabling and Inhibiting Health in PE Practices (adapted and developed from Harris & Almond, 1991)

Enabling Practices	Inhibiting Practices
Setting attainable tasks and challenges	Setting decontextualised tasks
	Exposing student incompetence
Rewarding effort and improvement	Rewarding performance only
Encouraging and valuing students' contributions	Treating students as 'empty vessels'
Offering variety and choice of activities	Enforcing monotonous or repetitive drills
Offering activities which can be pursued beyond the curriculum during extra-curricular time and/or in the local community (i.e. which have 'carry over' potential)	Offering meaningless, irrelevant activities with no 'carry over' potential
Encouraging independent learning and involving students in decision making	Keeping students dependent on the teacher and the teachers' decisions
Asking students if they wish to share work	Demanding students display their work
Ensuring fair competition against others	Allowing unfair competition against others

practical knowledge base. Given PE is, by definition, a physical subject this statement may seem like common sense. However, evidence suggests some teaching of health and health-related concepts is overly theoretical and classroom-based which is at odds with the physical nature of the subject. Learning about health through active participation provides an opportunity to introduce young people to an extensive range of activities, contributes positively to young people's physical activity levels and can promote understanding and development of key transferable skills such as decision making and evaluating (Cale & Harris, 2019).

While philosophical strides in PE have clearly been made in recent years and many of these principles and the enabling practices outlined should now be well embedded in PE practice, as Chapters 1 and 3 reveal, there are still some challenges and questionable practices in the area which may be hindering efforts to achieve policy and curricular expectations and positively influence the lifestyles of young people.

Box 2.1 Health in PE Philosophy, Principles and Practices

Reflect on your own knowledge and/or experiences of health-related learning in PE and consider the following questions:

1   To what extent is 'every child'/student at the heart of the PE curriculum in your school? Consider the reasons for your answer.
2   Do you and your colleagues adopt the enabling practices and avoid the inhibiting practices when teaching health in PE?
3   Can you identify any more health-related enabling (to adopt) and/or inhibiting practices (to avoid)?

Learning Underpinning Health

Despite the promotion of health being a key aim and component of PE in many countries, detailed references to health-related learning in statutory curricula appear to be limited. For example, in England, although health has featured within successive versions of the National Curriculum for PE (Department for Education, 2013), specific requirements or guidance relating to health-related learning outcomes and activities in the programmes of study remain lacking (Cale & Harris, 2018). This is clearly not helpful for teachers who are left to interpret the requirements and determine what health-related learning should look like for themselves (Cale, 2021) and then plan a meaningful, coherent and progressive health-related curriculum to achieve these requirements.

To start with, the health knowledge, skills and experiences young people require to be able to successfully engage in a healthy, active lifestyle need to be identified. In recognition of this and in the absence of any real guidance, health-related outcomes for children aged 5–16 years have been developed. These were first published in 2000 (Harris, 2000) and recently updated (Harris & Cale, 2019). The initial outcomes represented the collective efforts of a working group comprising representatives of national PE, sport and health organisations who sought to establish some consensus on health-related learning to support PE teachers in the area. There was widespread agreement that the outcomes needed to focus on all domains of learning, including the cognitive (knowledge and understanding), behavioural and affective, alongside the physical, and that learning should take place in and through a range of sport, dance and physical activity experiences including individualised lifetime and recreational activities. To illustrate this scope and breadth of learning, the outcomes were thus designed to include cognitive, behavioural and affective components and organised within four categories or areas: safety issues, exercise effects, health benefits and activity promotion. Furthermore, they were differentiated by National Curriculum age group (i.e. 5–7 years; 7–11 years; 11–14 years and 14–16 years) to show progression in learning with age. The full set of outcomes are published elsewhere (see Harris & Cale, 2019) but a few examples for each age range and category are summarised in Table 2.2.

Table 2.2 Exemplars of Health-Related Learning Outcomes (adapted from Harris & Cale, 2019)

	5–7 Age Range	*7–11 Age Range*	*11–14 Age Range*	*14–16 Age Range*
Safety issues	Explain that activity starts with a gentle warm up and finishes with a calming cool down	Identify the purpose of warming up and cooling down and describe the parts of a warm up and cool down	Explain the purpose of and plan and perform each component of a warm up and cool down	Evaluate warm ups and cool downs and take responsibility for safe and effective preparation for and recovery from activity

(*Continued*)

	5–7 Age Range	7–11 Age Range	11–14 Age Range	14–16 Age Range
Exercise effects	Recognise, describe and feel the effects of activity, including changes to: breathing, heart rate, appearance and feelings	Explain and feel the short-term effects of activity, e.g. breathing and heart rate increases to provide and pump more oxygen to working muscles	Explain and monitor a range of short-term effects of activity on the cardiovascular and musculoskeletal systems	Explain that training programmes develop health-related and skill-related components of fitness
Health benefits	Explain that regular activity improves health by helping body parts to grow, develop and work well and by helping one to feel good	Explain that activity strengthens bones and muscles, helps keep joints flexible, and can be fun and social	Explain a range of long-term benefits of activity such as reduced risk of heart disease, osteoporosis and obesity and that activity can improve mental health and social and psychological well-being, e.g. by spending time with friends, reducing anxiety	Explain that frequent and appropriate activity enhances the physical, social and psychological well-being of all individuals including the young and old, able-bodied and disabled, and those with health conditions
Activity promotion	Identify when, where and how they can be active at school (in and out of lessons)	Identify when, where and how they can be active in school and outside	Access information about a range of activity opportunities at school, home and in the local community and identify ways of incorporating activity into their lifestyles	Access physical activity personnel such as coaches/ instructors and facilities and services such as leisure centres, sport clubs and courses in the local community

---

Box 2.2 Health-Related Learning Outcomes

Reflect on the learning outcomes in Table 2.2 and your own knowledge and/or experiences of health-related learning in PE and consider the following questions:

1 To what extent does each category (safety; exercise effects; health benefits; activity promotion) feature in the PE curriculum?
2 Do any categories receive little or no coverage and do any receive excessive coverage? If so, why do you think this is? Is this potentially problematic for students?
3 Can you identify the progression in learning within each category and from one age range to the next? Why is such progression important?

Despite the breadth of the health-related learning outcomes, research has found that outcomes related to safety issues and exercise effects are given more attention in practice than those associated with health benefits and activity promotion (Cale & Harris, 2018; Harris & Leggett, 2015). In other words, there is more focus on the 'physical' and 'instrumental' outcomes concerned with health and on the 'physical body' (Quennerstedt, 2019) which it has been suggested leads to many teachers adopting narrow approaches in their teaching of health (Alfrey & Gard, 2014). Reasons for this focus are likely due to PE teachers' previous studies and training which have increasingly tended to emphasise the hard sciences, the physical body and quantitative evaluation, a phenomenon which has been referred to as the 'scientisation' of PE (Alfrey & Gard, 2019; Kirk, 2010). Plus, in the absence of any real steer, PE teachers unsurprisingly fall back on what they know and feel comfortable teaching (Cale, 2021). While all categories and outcomes have a place in the PE curriculum, those which focus on health benefits and activity promotion are the ones that are most closely associated with lifelong engagement in physical activity (Cale & Harris, 2018) and should therefore be given just as much attention.

Also important to recognise when considering health-related learning is how young people are increasingly exposed to and actively engage with and share health information and messages from various sources, including the media and social media (see Chapter 7). Despite the potential benefits of so much information being at young people's fingertips, the danger is that it is often not censored or quality assured, and may therefore be of poor quality, inaccurate or advocate questionable or even harmful behaviours and practices. Similarly, there has been a rapid growth in the availability of health-related digital technologies (Casey, Goodyear & Armour, 2017) and most notably apps and wearables which are likely to be attractive and motivating to many young people. Again though, while such technologies may offer benefits, a concern is their tendency to 'quantify' and focus on the narrow physical and instrumental aspects of health. This could lead to young people simply adopting and repeating easily described behaviours (Goodyear, Kerner & Quennerstedt, 2019) or obsessive surveillance and monitoring practices and behaviours (Rich & Miah, 2017; Williamson, 2015).

In light of these developments, young people need to be equipped with the knowledge and skills to become critical consumers of health-related information, messages and resources, including digital technologies (Cale, 2021; Macdonald, Enright & McCuaig, 2018). Close attention to the pedagogical principles and philosophy outlined earlier as well as to the adoption of a socially critical perspective to teaching and learning about health is key to achieving this. Indeed, the need for socially critical and alternative perspectives has been acknowledged for some time (Kirk, 2006) and it is encouraging to see progress being made in the context of health and PE in this respect. For example, as touched on in Chapter 1, the new 'futures-oriented' Health and PE curriculum in Australia (ACARA, 2012) has reportedly shifted to a curriculum underpinned by a focus on educative outcomes, the development of health literacy skills, learning in, about and through movement, and a critical enquiry-based approach (Macdonald, Enright & McCuaig, 2018). Likewise, there has been a shift in the curriculum in New Zealand, away from the traditional fitness, team sport and biomedical focus (Burrows, 1999, cited in Dyson, Landi & Gordon, 2018) towards well-being, with attitudes and values, health promotion and a socio-ecological perspective guiding learning (Ministry of Education, 2007).

There is clearly a need for a broad, balanced, holistic and critical approach to health-related learning which pays good and equal attention to the full range of outcomes, all domains of learning, and which strives to equip and empower young people with the knowledge, skills and confidence to make informed decisions regarding their physical activity participation and behaviour.

The Organisation of Health in PE

Just as there has been uncertainty underpinning the learning associated with health in PE, questions have also remained about the organisation of the area. Two main approaches to the organisation of health in PE have been identified and critiqued in the literature, an integrated or a focussed approach (Cale & Harris, 2009; Murdoch & Whitehead, 2010). The first involves integrating health-related learning through traditional activities such as athletics, dance, games, gymnastics, outdoor education and swimming. Thus, units of learning and the associated lessons develop learning about health alongside learning other PE areas and content. Alternatively, the focussed approach involves teaching health through discrete separate units on health. These units are often given a variety of names such as health-related exercise or health-related fitness and comprise lessons with an explicit focus on learning about health.

Examples of both approaches are provided in Tables 2.3 and 2.4, which include selected learning outcomes and learning activities to illustrate how health-related learning can be incorporated through both. The integrated approach (Table 2.3) focusses on dance and health-relating learning outcomes related to safety issues and activity promotion, whilst the focussed approach (Table 2.4) centres on cardiovascular exercise (CV) and learning outcomes related to health benefits, exercise effects and safety.

There is no right or wrong approach and each has its merits as well as drawbacks. For example, the main strengths of an integrated approach are that health-related learning is seen as related and integral to all PE experiences and all physical activities are recognised as contributing towards health (Harris, 2000; Murdoch & Whitehead, 2010). On the other hand, a limitation is that by integrating health-related learning with the teaching of traditional PE activities health may be overlooked or marginalised at the expense of skill development or tactical understanding (Cale & Harris, 2018). Equally, students may be confused about or not able to clearly identify the focus for learning in an integrated lesson. The focussed approach avoids the above limitations, and also has the advantage of moving away from a traditional, activity-based curriculum to enable units and lessons to incorporate a broader range of activities and health-related learning. A drawback of the approach, however, is that separate units of learning or lessons on health could infer that the area is not closely related to other learning and elements of PE (Murdoch & Whitehead, 2010).

Table 2.3 Example Integrated Approach – Learning about Health through Dance

Learning Outcomes	Learning Activities
Dance Students should be able to: • Identify and explain the key characteristics of street dance as a particular style of dance • Perform a warm up and motif in the style of street dance • Develop a street dance motif using appropriate actions and dynamic features. **Health** Students should be able to: • Explain the importance of warming up before taking part in physical activity, and specifically dance, and identify and explain the purpose of the different components of a warm up (safety issues) • Plan and evaluate the effectiveness of a dance warm up (*safety issues*) • Access information about the dance opportunities available to them at school, at home and in the local community (*activity promotion*).	**Introduction** Students are introduced to the dual focus and learning outcomes of the lesson: (1) Dance styles and specifically street dance; (2) Learning about health through dance. **Teacher Question and Answer** What is a warm up? Why do we need to warm up before exercise? **Warm Up** Students are introduced to the three main parts of a warm up (mobility exercises; cardiovascular/pulse raising activities, and short static stretches) and led through selected warm up activities in keeping with the style of street dance. As they perform these, they are asked to reflect on the purpose of each part of the warm up. **Planning and Evaluating a Warm up** In pairs, students devise a short warm up incorporating some of the movements introduced earlier plus ideas of their own. Students perform their warm up to another pair who evaluate it according to given success criteria. For example, did you spot the different parts of the warm up?; which mobility, cardiovascular/pulse-raising, and stretching exercises were included?; was the warm up effective in preparing the body for the activity to follow? **Performing a Street Dance Motif** Students learn, practise and refine a set street dance motif which comprises actions typical of the style.

While practising and refining the motif, students are asked to reflect on the characteristics of street dance in terms of: actions, dynamics, spatial and relationship features. Students discuss their reflections/observations with a partner.

Teacher Question and Answer

What actions are typically performed in street dance? How are the actions typically performed?

Where are actions typically performed? With whom are the actions typically performed?

Developing a Street Dance Motif

In pairs students develop the motif using action features, by adding: (i) a movement involving a body part isolation; (ii) a very energetic/ explosive movement; (iii) an acrobatic element and/or a point of contact between dancers.

The additions should communicate the dynamics and intention and style of the dance. Students then link the two motifs together and perform the whole dance through.

Cool Down

Following the above, students perform a suitable cool-down.

Plenary Teacher Question and Answer

If interested in taking part in and learning more about dance, what opportunities are available at school/at home/locally?

Where can you find out about the dance opportunities available?

Table 2.4 Example Focussed Approach – Cardiovascular Exercise

Learning Outcomes	Learning Activities
Students should be able to: • Explain what cardiovascular (CV) exercise is and its importance to health (*health benefits*) • Explain the key teaching/technique points and key principles underpinning safe and effective CV exercise (*safety*) • Perform a range of CV exercises safely and with good technique (safety; exercise effects) • Plan and perform a short exercise routine or circuit which: (i) includes a variety of exercises; (ii) works the CV system (*exercise effects*)	**Introductory Teacher Question and Answer** What is CV exercise? Can you name some CV activities? Why is CV exercise important to health? **Warm Up** Lead students through various CV exercises which start gently and gradually increase in intensity, demonstrating, highlighting and giving feedback regarding the technique for each. **Teacher Question and Answer** What are the key teaching/technique points for performing different CV exercises? What are some of the key safety considerations when performing CV exercise? **Perform a Range of CV Exercises** Lead students through a selection of other CV exercises/activities asking them to focus on performing the exercises safely and with good technique. For example, skipping, circuits or aerobic routines which involve whole body exercises, an element of choice, and which can be sustained. **Teacher Question and Answer** What did you notice about the exercises/activities? Why is it sensible to vary the exercise/activities? What might happen if we perform CV exercise with poor technique and/or don't follow safe practice?

Planning and Performing an Exercise Routine or Circuit

Working in small groups, students draw on any of the exercises/ activities already performed (or other ideas they may have), to plan a short exercise routine or circuit which: (i) includes a variety of exercises/activities; (ii) works the CV system.

Students then perform their routine/ circuit paying attention to good exercise technique and safe practice.

Cool Down

Students cool down with some gentle CV exercise and static stretches of the main muscle groups.

Given the above, a combined approach to teaching health in PE has been recommended as it builds on the strengths of each, helps to reinforce and promote consistency and coherence in health-related learning, provides scope for more adequately addressing the knowledge base underpinning health, and enables links to be made to other PE and physical activity experiences (Cale & Harris, 2009). As noted in Chapter 1, opportunities also exist to connect, reinforce and broaden health-related learning by making links with other curriculum areas. For example, a topic approach can be taken which involves identifying a specific health topic or theme and coordinating coverage of this across relevant curriculum subjects. Thus, the topic of energy could be addressed in PE (in terms of the role of exercise in energy balance), Food Technology (in terms of healthy eating), and in Science (measuring energy input and output; understanding metabolism). While the most obvious cross-curricular opportunities lie with Personal, Social and Health Education, Science and Food Technology, with some thought and mapping virtually all curriculum areas can contribute to health-related learning in meaningful ways. This combined and cross-subject approach furthermore aligns with the whole-school approach to health (introduced in Chapter 1 and discussed in Chapter 4) which is increasingly being advocated within and beyond the UK (McMullen et al., 2015).

Clearly though, PE teachers are in the best position to make professional judgements concerning the organisation of health in (and beyond) their PE curriculum based on the strengths, limitations and opportunities of each approach, and their school context and students' needs. The critical issue should be the effectiveness of the learning more than the particular approach(es) adopted (Cale & Harris, 2009).

Box 2.3 Approaches to the Organisation of Health in PE

Reflect on the different approaches to organising the teaching of health in PE.

1   How is health-related learning organised in PE in your department? Which approach(es) do you adopt and why? How successful do you feel these to be?
2   Which areas of health-related learning do, or could, you cover via which approach(es)?

Conclusion

This chapter has explored some of the fundamental considerations and pedagogical principles underpinning the teaching of health in PE, including its philosophy, content, outcomes and organisation. For the teaching of health in PE to be effective, a pedagogical emphasis and knowledge base which puts the 'child' at the core, rather than the activity or curriculum is advocated. These should be underpinned by positive messages and practices focussed on physical activity for life, experiential learning, the acquisition of a practical knowledge base, and an explicit commitment to inclusion, equity, democracy and empowerment. In recognition of a narrow approach to the teaching of health in PE and the range of health-related information, messages and practices young people are exposed to from other sources, the chapter has also highlighted the need for a broad, balanced, holistic and critical approach to health-related learning in order to equip and empower young people to make informed decisions regarding their physical activity participation and behaviour. Two main approaches to the organisation of health in PE were identified and critiqued, an integrated and focussed approach, but it was acknowledged that the critical issue informing which approach(es) to adopt should be the effectiveness of the learning. Throughout the chapter, teachers have been encouraged to reflect on the teaching, health-related learning and organisation of health in their own PE curricula and we hope that by doing so, some positive actions and outcomes both for teachers and students will result.

Summary and Recommendations

- For the teaching of health in PE to be effective, a pedagogical emphasis and knowledge base is advocated which puts the 'child' at the core, rather than the activity or curriculum.
- Key philosophical principles and messages underpinning health in PE include that physical activity is for all and for life, everyone can be good at and benefit from physical activity and can find the right kind of physical activity for them, and excellence in physical activity is maintaining an active way of life.
- Underpinning health in PE should be an explicit commitment to inclusion, equity, democracy, empowerment, a refocussing towards physical activity for life, and teaching comprising experiential learning and the acquisition of a practical knowledge base.
- References to health-related learning and to specific outcomes and health-related activities within statutory curricula are often limited, leaving questions over how health-related curricula aims are to be achieved and health-related curriculum developed.
- In recognition of the above and to illustrate the scope and breadth of learning, health-related outcomes for children have been published which cover cognitive, behavioural and affective domains of learning, alongside physical, and address safety issues, exercise effects, health benefits and activity promotion.
- Research has found that health-related learning outcomes related to safety issues and exercise effects are given more attention than those associated with health benefits and activity promotion, yet it is the latter which are most closely associated with lifelong engagement in physical activity.
- A broad, balanced, holistic and critical approach to health-related learning is needed which pays good and equal attention to the full range of outcomes, all domains of learning, and which strives to equip and empower young people to make informed decisions regarding their physical activity participation and behaviour.
- There are two main approaches to the organisation of health in PE, an integrated and focussed approach, each of which has

merits and drawbacks, though a combined approach which builds on the strengths of each is recommended.

- PE teachers are in the best position to make professional judgements concerning the organisation of health in PE, with the critical issue being the effectiveness of the learning more than the particular approach(es) adopted.

Box 2.4 Next Steps

Based on the content of this chapter and with respect to the teaching of health in PE in your school, reflect on the following:

1   Pedagogical principles and practices
2   Learning
3   Organisation.

Identify 1–2 specific actions for each (and a timeline for implementing these) which you feel will have a positive impact on: (i) your teaching of health and (ii) your students.

Bibliography

Harris, J., & Cale, L. (2019). *Promoting Active Lifestyles in Schools*. Champaign, IL: Human Kinetics.

References

Alfrey, L., Cale, L., & Webb, L.A. (2012). Physical education teachers' continuing professional development in health-related exercise. *Physical Education and Sport Pedagogy*, 17(5), 477–491.

Alfrey, L., & Gard, M. (2014). A crack where the light gets in: A study of health and physical education teachers' perspectives on fitness testing as a context for learning about health. *Asia-Pacific Journal of Health, Sport and Physical Education*, 5(1), 3–18.

Alfrey, L., & Gard, M. (2019). Figuring out the prevalence of fitness testing in physical education: A figurational analysis. *European Physical Education Review*, 25(1), 187–202.

Armour, K., & Harris, J. (2013). Making the case for developing new PE-for-health pedagogies. *Quest*, 65(2), 201–219.

Australian Curriculum, Assessment and Reporting Authority (ACARA). (2012). *The Health and Physical Education Curriculum F-10*. Sydney: ACARA.

Burrows, L. (1999). *Developmental Discourses in School Physical Education.* Wollongong, NSW: University of Wollongong.

Cale, L. (2021). Physical education's journey on the road to health. *Sport, Education and Society*, 26(5), 486–499.

Cale, L., & Harris, J. (2009). *Getting the Buggers Fit.* 2nd edn. London: Continuum.

Cale, L., & Harris, J. (2018). The role of knowledge and understanding in fostering physical literacy. *Journal of Teaching in Physical Education*, 37(3), 280–287.

Casey, A., Goodyear, V.A., & Armour, K.M. (2017). Rethinking the relationship between pedagogy, technology and learning in health and physical education. *Sport, Education and Society*, 22(2), 288–304.

Department for Education. (2013). *National Curriculum in England: Physical Education Programmes of Study.* London: Department for Education.

Dyson, B., Landi, D., & Gordin, B. (2018). Redesign of PE in Aotearoa New Zealand. In H.A. Lawson (Ed.), *Redesigning Physical Education. An Equity Agenda in which every Child Matters* (pp. 182–195). Oxon: Routledge.

Elbourn, J., & James, A. (2013). *Fitness Room Activities for Secondary Schools. A Guide to Promoting Effective Learning about Healthy Active Lifestyles.* Leeds, UK: Coachwise.

Goodyear, V., Kerner, C., & Quennerstedt, M. (2019). Young people's uses of wearable healthy lifestyle technologies; surveillance, self-surveillance and resistance. *Sport, Education and Society*, 24(3), 212–225.

Harris, J. (2000). *Health-related Exercise in the National Curriculum.* Leeds: Human Kinetics.

Harris, J., & Almond, L. (1991). Learning to care. *The Bulletin of Physical Education*, 27(1), 5–11.

Harris, J., & Cale, L. (2019). *Promoting Active Lifestyles in Schools.* Leeds: Human Kinetics.

Harris, J., & Leggett, G. (2015). Influences on the expression of health within physical education curricula in secondary schools in England and Wales. *Sport, Education and Society*, 20(7), 908–923.

Kirk, D. (2006). The obesity 'crisis' and school physical education. *Sport, Education and Society*, 11(2), 121–133.

Kirk, D. (2010). Four relational issues and the bigger picture. In: D. Kirk. *Physical Education Futures* (pp. 97–120). Abingdon, Oxon: Routledge.

Macdonald, D., Enright, E., & McCuaig, L. (2018). Re-visioning the Australian curriculum for health and physical education. In H.A. Lawson (Ed.), *Redesigning Physical Education. An Equity Agenda in which Every Child Matters* (pp. 196–209). Oxon: Routledge.

McMullen, J., Ni Chroinin, D., Tammelin, T., Pogorzelska, M., & Van Der Mars, J. (2015) International approaches to whole-of-school physical activity promotion. *Quest*, 67(4), 384–399.

Ministry of Education. (2007). *The New Zealand Curriculum.* Wellington, New Zealand: Learning Media.

Murdoch, E., & Whitehead, M. (2010). Physical literacy, fostering the attributes and curriculum planning. In M. Whitehead (Ed.), *Physical Literacy: Throughout the Lifecourse* (pp. 175–188). London, UK: Routledge.

Quennerstedt, M. (2019). Healthying physical education – On the possibility of learning health. *Physical Education and Sport Pedagogy*, 24(1), 1–15.

Rich, E., & Miah, A. (2017). Mobile, wearable and ingestible health technologies: Towards a critical research agenda. *Health Sociology Review*, 26(1), 84–97.

Williamson, B. (2015). Algorithmic skin: Health-tracking technologies, personal analytics and the biopedagogies of digitized health and physical education. *Sport, Education and Society*, 20(1), 133–151.

3 Fitness Testing as a Debated and Contested PE-for-Health Practice

Laura Alfrey and Dillon Landi

Introduction

A number of PE-for-health practices have been the focus of debate over the years, such as cross-country, but few are more contested than fitness testing. While fitness is merely one component of health, research from England (Alfrey, Cale & Webb, 2012; Cale & Harris, 2009) and Australia (Alfrey & Gard, 2014) suggests fitness testing is the most frequently used context for learning about health within PE, and thus is classified as a 'PE-for-health' practice. To examine fitness testing, we draw on existing international research before sharing and analysing a case study which exemplifies how fitness testing, and PE more broadly, can affect the multiple dimensions of learners' bodies and health. While it is recognised the perspectives and approaches shared here could never apply to all teachers and learners, they do provide a basis for reflecting on fitness testing as a contested PE-for-health practice and exploring alternative testing approaches.

The tendency to test, measure, describe and categorise children's bodies is not a new phenomenon. This tradition can be traced back to the start of the twentieth century (Kirk, 1998) where measuring children formed part of health inspection regimes that occurred across the Anglosphere (Alfrey & Gard, 2014). By the 1950s, links were made between health and physical activity, and we saw the emergence of, for example, the President's Council on Youth Fitness in the United States of America (USA) (Freedson, Cureton & Heath, 2000), the Australian Youth Fitness Survey (Willee, 1973) and the English National Child Measurement Programme (Public Health England, 2013).

Fitness testing as a PE-for-health practice remains a persistent feature of PE programmes internationally, especially in countries such as England, Australia and the USA. The popularity of fitness testing within PE, however, has been contested for decades, with the main

DOI: 10.4324/9781003225904-3

arguments of the debate centred on a few key questions: (i) why do teachers carry out fitness testing?; (ii) how do teachers carry out fitness testing?; and (iii) how are learners experiencing fitness testing? In this chapter we share some evidence-based responses to each of these questions to provide insight into why fitness testing continues to be a debated PE-for-health practice.

After reading this chapter, you will be able to:

i   articulate key debates concerning the teaching of fitness testing;
ii reflect on and critique your own practices related to fitness testing;
iii plan for educative and inclusive approaches to fitness testing within a broader fitness education unit.

Why Do Teachers Carry out Fitness Testing?

In the USA, Keating and Silverman (2004) surveyed over 300 PE teachers and found three main reasons for including fitness testing in programmes: (1) to promote physical activity and health; (2) to record students' progress and (3) to assess and/or improve teachers' physical activity and fitness instruction. More recently, Alfrey and Gard (2014) surveyed (n=108) and interviewed (n=8) Australian PE teachers to understand why fitness testing was the main context/activity through which health was taught in PE. The findings revealed the three most popular reasons for carrying out fitness testing were: (1) to motivate children to be physically active and promote health; (2) fitness testing is an 'easy' lesson to teach; (3) fitness testing is a traditional practice in PE.

Thus, research suggests the most common rationale for PE teachers carrying out fitness testing include:

- *Health/fitness/physical activity promotion*: This rationale is well-intentioned but there is no evidence to suggest fitness testing promotes health, fitness or physical activity. There is, however, evidence to suggest fitness testing can negatively impact future health, fitness and physical activity (Ladwig, Vazou & Ekkekakis, 2018).
- *Assessment*: In some schools, fitness test results are used to assess achievement in PE. This is problematic given that fitness testing does not measure student learning.
- *Tradition*: History is a powerful predictor of current and future practices in education. Tradition alone, though, is not a suitable rationale to continue such a contested practice that often lacks educative value.

Moving more towards a focus on learning in, through and about fitness testing, would represent a stronger and more appropriate rationale for its inclusion within PE.

Box 3.1 Reflections and Thoughts on Fitness Testing in PE

Reflect on your own knowledge and/or experiences of fitness testing in PE and consider the following questions:

1   To what extent does fitness testing feature in your school's PE curriculum? What are the reasons for your answer?
2   Why might you, as a PE teacher, need to assess students' fitness levels?
3   What knowledge and skills do you expect students to demonstrate after participating in fitness testing?

How Do Teachers Implement Fitness Testing?

There is limited research on how teachers implement fitness testing, but most accounts suggest a typical lesson involves students completing a battery of fitness tests such as the beep test, Cooper 12-minute run, sit and reach and the Illinois agility test. When asked what a typical fitness testing lesson looked like in their school, one Australian secondary teacher stated:

> I carry out fitness testing twice per year. I do the beep test, basketball throw, sit and reach, 1.6 km run, height, weight, shoulder stretch, sit ups. I do it because it is set out in our school's curriculum that students should do fitness testing at the beginning of term 1 and beginning of term 4.
>
> (Alfrey & Gard, 2014, p. 10)

As the above quotation suggests, it is commonplace for fitness testing to occur at the start and end of the school year, with the expectation that improvement across different dimensions of fitness will occur in the interim. Such improvement is not always possible, however, due to a range of factors (e.g. genetics, geographical location, lack of social support etc.). Equally, if students naturally grow, their scores are likely to improve.

Research internationally has problematised how fitness testing is taught. Some key debates concerning the teaching of fitness testing are:

- *Fitness testing or fitness education?* Fitness testing often occurs in a single lesson, disconnected from broader fitness education programmes (Simonton, Mercier & Garn, 2019) and with unclear educative aims (Hopple & Graham, 1995; Placek et al., 2001). Embedding testing within a fitness education unit may support learners in planning, enacting and evaluating a fitness programme.
- *Are students on display?* When students participate in fitness tests in front of others, often for pragmatic and logistical reasons, this results in negative affect (emotions and feelings), especially for learners who are considered 'poor performers' (Zhu et al., 2018).
- *How are results used?* Research suggests fitness test results are rarely used to support education (Simonton, Mercier & Garn, 2019). What happens with results is not always clear. This issue has become problematic in some places because data privacy laws protecting minors are stringent. In fact, parents in one state in the USA successfully argued against the implementation of third-party private fitness assessments (like FitnessGRAM®) because school districts shared personal student records and violated data protection laws.

Box 3.2 Previous Fitness Testing Practices

Reflect on previous fitness testing practices and consider the following questions:

1   What is the value of understanding fitness and health concepts?
2   How could fitness and health concepts be taught without putting student bodies on display, emphasising fitness scores?
3   Why is using fitness test scores not an appropriate way to assess student achievement in (non-examinable) PE?

How Do Learners Experience Fitness Testing?

All learners experience fitness testing in different ways. O'Keeffe, MacDoncha and Donnelly (2021, p. 53) suggest 'analysing students' attitudes and experiences (of fitness testing) is a critical step in developing evidence-based pedagogical approaches'. Their research from Ireland found learners, and particularly boys, tended to have positive attitudes towards fitness testing and viewed it as a useful part of PE. It seems two key factors contributed to these positive learner attitudes: (1) testing was one component of a broader fitness education unit, giving students an opportunity to learn in, through and about fitness testing; and (2) a student-centred approach to fitness testing, whereby learners with seniority facilitated the administration of the tests, served to support the learning and process more broadly.

O'Keeffe and colleagues' (2021) study highlights the importance of considering pedagogical approaches to fitness testing. Other research suggests more common pedagogical approaches to fitness testing (e.g. whole-class beep test, public displaying of scores) can cause distress for some students. Indeed, Lodewyk and Sullivan (2016) argued fitness testing can negatively impact learner body image, anxiety and self-esteem while Ladwig, Vazou and Ekkekakis (2018) reported negative affective experiences from fitness testing during childhood lasted into adulthood, thus negatively impacting lifelong physical activity. This should perhaps come as no surprise as we have long been warned this may be the case for some learners. In 2008, Garrett and Wrench claimed 'the continuing and unproblematic use of fitness testing in schools and universities might actually contribute to narrow learning outcomes that cause more pain than pleasure' (2008, p. 21).

As teachers, we need to be mindful of the impact our practices have on learners and work with them to develop safe, educative and pleasurable physical activity experiences. With this in mind, we next rethink how 'health' is understood in PE by sharing a case study.

Rethinking 'Health' in PE: 'What the Body Can Do'

In rethinking 'health' in PE, we suggest moving beyond describing 'what the body is' (e.g. underweight, flexible, strong) and instead focus on 'what the body can do' (Fox, 2012). This approach helps us to reconsider the role of fitness testing in PE and respond to the debates concerning its practices. The shift to thinking about 'what the body can do' allows for learners to be seen from a multi-dimensional and holistic perspective.

Historically, the word 'health' in PE has referred to processes of 'schooling bodies' (Kirk, 1998) to: (a) reproduce privileged body types

(Tinning, 1985); (b) increase public health outcomes (McKenzie & Lounsbery, 2009) and (c) promote attainment of motor and sport skills (Tucker, Bebeley & Conteh, 2017). As such, young bodies have been reduced to and restricted by labels that describe their body type (e.g. skinny, obese), level of physical activity (e.g. low, moderate, vigorous), or skill development (e.g. basic, intermediate, advanced). Rather than seeing 'health' as a description of 'what the body is', we shift our understanding of health towards 'what the body can do'. There are several benefits to doing this. First, our field can shift away from pathologising and categorising bodies as 'healthy', 'unhealthy', 'fit' or 'at-risk' and instead value and include all bodies. Second, descriptions often focus on and over-emphasise the biological/physical body. The body, however, can be understood from a range of perspectives including sociological, psychological, political and anthropological (Fox, 2012). These perspectives are interconnected and just as important as the physical body. By re-imagining health as 'what the body can do' in PE, we can consider the body's capability across different dimensions (e.g. psychological, social, physical). Historically, PE has siloed different dimensions but we recognise that 'what the body can do' is dependent on the network of relations *between* dimensions. In other words, the relations between the physical, social, psychological, emotional and so forth empower and limit 'what the body can do' in PE.

From this multi-dimensional perspective, if cultural, social, psychological and physical aspects of the body have *positive* relationships with each other during movement, then these will enhance the body's ability and motivation to move and learn. If one of these relationships falters however (e.g. through injury or stress), this will limit the body's ability to move and learn. 'What the body can do' therefore, is both enhanced and limited by a network of relationships both internal and external to the body.

If we understand health and the body as multi-dimensional, then PE should be concerned with learning experiences that promote positive relationships between the different dimensions of the body. 'Health' from this perspective, and in the context of PE, goes beyond pathology (free from disease) and is evaluated by the body's ability to enter into as many new positive relationships as possible (e.g. learning new skills, learning fitness concepts). Therefore, the goal of PE (and health) is to expand 'what the body can do'.

We now share a case study of Elena[1] and her experiences of PE and fitness testing, before analysing this to address the question 'How did Elena's PE experiences affect what her body could do?'

Case Study: Elena, PE and Fitness Testing

Elena is a 15-year-old Spanish girl who lives in Aotearoa New Zealand. She identifies as a cisgender woman with a queer sexuality. She is an active young person who plays competitive volleyball and netball at her school. Despite being a sportsperson, she expressed 'hatred' for PE. She dislikes PE due to the monotonous, repetitive nature of the content, focus on fitness, and how she feels about her body ('fat' and 'slow'). Elena describes herself as a 'bigger' girl with 'Spanish hips' and 'Rugby thighs', although she readily admits to never playing (or wanting to play) rugby.

In PE, Elena had to weigh herself and calculate and track her BMI using graphs and tables. To improve her fitness scores, Elena participated in daily runs in class where she was instructed to complete laps at her own pace. Doing the laps generated an emotional response for Elena. She commented:

> People are overtaking and lapping you and you are like 'OK'. I get you're not supposed to compare, but come on. It's horrible because I don't want to think about myself in bad ways but everyone is always better than me.

Elena described doing a battery of fitness tests in PE (e.g. beep test, sit and reach). She noted it was obvious who was going to do well (or not) during testing. As such, Elena worked with girls of similar fitness levels, and they agreed to leave the beep test at the same time to avoid being bullied. After ending the tests early, they hung out together and bonded over being 'not as fit as the rest of the class'. Elena is required to wear a uniform for PE; she stated, 'Oh my god, the uniforms are tight fitting, and I don't want my classmates seeing me'. One of the reasons she didn't want to wear a uniform was because of gender norms. She said, 'As a girl I am supposed to look a certain way and wear certain clothes and have a certain body in PE'. What's worse is that when some girls did not 'fit in' to gender norms they were ridiculed by classmates, 'They won't say anything to your face, but they will call you a lesbian behind your back'. Such comments made Elena feel bad about her body, fitness, and identity.

In discussing PE and her teachers, Elena stated:

> They want people to be sporty and active. They want us to care about things like fitness and stuff. But they don't understand that health is more than just like running and keeping physically fit. It's about so much more than that.

Elena went on to explain that in her family, being healthy means being able to dance and celebrate during events. It also means expressing who you are and feeling good about yourself. Or, as she stated, 'It's about being in a community where you don't have to feel isolated. You can feel safe, meet people, play games, be who you are, and learn from others'.

Box 3.3 Elena's Story

Reflect on Elena's story:

1   Do Elena's feelings and experiences towards PE surprise you? Do you think other young people may feel similarly about PE?
2   How might Elena's experiences in fitness testing and PE impact 'what her body can do' within and beyond school?
3   If you were Elena's PE teacher, what might you do differently?

In considering the question: how did Elena's PE experiences impact what her body could do?, we consider the ways in which these experiences enhanced as well as limited her body. We do not pass comment on whether the experiences were 'good or bad', 'healthy or unhealthy' or 'positive or negative' but examine the question via the cultural, psychological, social and physical dimensions of the body and health.

What Can the Cultural Body Do?

In the case study, Elena identified as a Spanish, queer 'thick' female athlete. Elena felt out of place and disenfranchised during fitness testing in PE. To start, the knowledge that underpins fitness testing comes from Western biomedical perspectives around exercise as a tool for 'optimal' physical health. This ran at odds with her Spanish cultural background where movement was aligned to bodily expressions, emotions and family relations. For Elena, fitness testing was detached from her culture and placed in a Western 'biomedical health' context that focussed on the individual.

Elena's ethnic identity also intersected with her other identities. For example, the tests often split learners by perceived gender. Elena explained how being a woman meant having lower testing expectations and specific clothing mandates. Such practices were aligned with cultural expectations placed on women's bodies, often limiting what they can do. When we consider the intersectionality of this situation, the big-hipped female body that is celebrated in Spanish and queer cultures is at odds with Western biomedical expectations within PE that value skinny bodies. The 'skinny' and 'toned' cultural expectations reinforced through fitness testing often made Elena feel like she did not 'fit in' to clothing or PE. Ultimately, this misalignment between Elena's identities and fitness testing practices and cultural norms limited what her body could do in PE.

What Can the Social Body Do?

The social body reflects the interpersonal relationships someone can enter into during PE. During her fitness testing experiences, Elena's social body was limited because her relationships were reduced to working with specific people. In other words, based on grouping and scoring, Elena formed social relationships with other learners who were either women and/or 'poor test performers'. From a teaching perspective this not only genders students but works to 'classify' and 'track' them into hierarchical groups based on fitness levels. This grouping limited Elena's body's ability to enter into interpersonal relationships with just a few classmates (female, low-skilled). Therefore, she may not have had similar experiences to those of boys and/or 'high performing' students.

The impact on Elena's social body was not all negative; her relations with a few peers could be considered positive. Despite being subjugated to lower status via cultural bodies (e.g. body size, gender, sexuality, test scores), the young women in Elena's story did not passively accept being treated poorly. Rather, they used their social relationships together to collude, drop out of and resist participating in fitness testing. Thus, while from one perspective it is clear these young diverse women did not learn much about fitness or enjoy fitness testing, from another perspective it could be argued they learnt how to work together to resist fitness testing practices. So, Elena's body may not have been able to enter into relationships that enhanced her fitness knowledge or ability, but she was able to enhance her ability to work with others and protest against dominant and discriminatory practices.

What Can the Psychological Body Do?

Through the case study we see a range of ways in which traditional approaches to fitness testing in PE can impact the 'psychological body'. Elena referred to her 'hate' for PE which seemed to have multiple roots and possible psychological effects. The ways in which PE was taught made her feel embarrassed of her 'big' and 'slow' body. Despite efforts by the teacher to protect students from comparison during fitness testing, the activity still prompted a psychological response for Elena because her performance was visible and comparable to both other classmates and scoring norms. Thus, she was forced to think of herself in 'negative ways'. As just noted, however, Elena also built relationships with other girls in her class which had a positive effect on her sense of self. Through the relationships she built with friends, in opposing fitness testing, Elena experienced an enhancement of her psychological body.

Looking beyond fitness testing, Elena's experiences prompt us to reconsider other contested practices such as compulsory uniforms. For Elena, the uniform she was required to wear made her feel embarrassed because her body deviated from 'the norm'. Moreover, her psychological body was harmed via the bullying she experienced, which reinforced her feelings of shame and embarrassment as well as threatened her identity as a cisgender Spanish, queer woman.

What Can the Physical Body Do?

Elena referred to the way in which fitness tests (e.g. beep test, Cooper run) were administered (i.e. in front of the whole class) revealing how these experiences impacted what her physical body could do. Elena's physical body was weighed and tracked under the gaze of her teacher and peers and based on her physical body she was categorised as a deviant, not conforming to gender or fitness norms. She was also required to cover her physical body with a compulsory and ill-fitting uniform. Moreover, she did not improve her fitness, nor did she feel physically good participating in exercise, further illustrating how fitness testing affected what Elena's physical body could do in PE.

Re-thinking Approaches to Fitness Testing: Expanding What the Body Can Do

In terms of alternatives to traditional fitness testing approaches, Vazou et al. (2019) suggest simple modifications to teaching could improve students' experiences of fitness testing. Drawing on research that focusses on fitness testing, what follows are some recommended approaches to teaching in, through and about fitness that can be educative, meaningful and safe for learners. When conducting fitness testing, we recommend teachers ensure they address all dimensions of the body. Notably, while these suggested practices are listed under 'one' dimension, many address multiple dimensions.

- The cultural body:
  - Ensure tests are meaningful to students' lives, identities and diverse cultures (e.g. youth culture, ethnic culture, gender culture).
  - Work with students to develop new assessments that are embedded by and teach about the diverse cultural groups that make up the community.
- The psychological body
  - Provide students the space to discuss the role fitness testing plays on how learners feel about themselves, their bodies and movement.
  - Have students analyse which forms of movement enhance their self-esteem and attitudes towards physical activity.
- The social body
  - Provide fitness testing opportunities that require students to work together, collaborate and develop meaningful connections with others.
  - Have students analyse how fitness testing practices may make other students who do not look like themselves feel in PE.
- The physical body
  - Have students engage in and consider how fitness testing can enhance different parts of their body (e.g. posture, muscular and cardiovascular systems).
  - Have students identify and develop one minor fitness goal and consider how their body changed as a result.
- The learning body
  - Make testing part of a broader fitness education curriculum/unit where the emphasis is on learning health and fitness concepts.
  - Do not rush fitness testing and provide time for students to explore, critique and learn about fitness testing through movement.

44 *Laura Alfrey and Dillon Landi*

In addition to the aforementioned bodily dimensions, we advocate paying attention to the 'reflective body'. This could be done by providing opportunities for students to reflect on their fitness testing experiences with regard to: (a) how testing makes them feel about their body and movement (psychological); (b) how their physical body feels and responds to movement (physical body); (c) what they have learnt (learning body); (d) the relevance of this practice in their lives (cultural) and (e) how movement can enhance personal relationships (social).

In terms of how tests are conducted, students themselves have suggested they would appreciate having an opportunity to choose:

- Where they are tested (e.g. at home, in school).
- Testing partners (e.g. three to five peers, friends).
- The tests they engage in, so they are relevant to their lives.
- To develop their own tests.

Students we have worked with have also been very clear that they:

- Want to know the purpose/learning goals of fitness testing.
- Do not want the focus to be the test scores.
- Do not want the results to be publicised.
- Want to know what happens to the results.

Conclusion

This chapter has examined fitness testing as a pervasive but contested feature of PE. Specifically, it has exemplified how fitness testing, and PE more broadly, can impact the multiple dimensions of students' bodies and health. We explored the value of moving beyond describing 'what the body is' and instead focussing on 'what the body can do' in PE. Doing so, we argue, aligns more closely with multi-dimensional understandings of health, and opens up opportunities for more inclusive PE-for-health practices. In response to ongoing debates related to fitness testing, we have shared some recommendations for the future of fitness testing in PE with a view to making it a more educative and inclusive experience for all students.

Summary and Recommendations

- A number of PE-for-health practices have been the focus of debate over the years, such as cross-country, but few are more contested than fitness testing.

- Fitness testing is the most frequently used context for learning about health within PE, and thus is classified as a 'PE-for-health' practice.
- The tendency to test, measure, describe and categorise children's bodies is not a new phenomenon. This tradition can be traced back to the start of the twentieth century.
- Teachers cite a range of reasons for including fitness testing in their PE programmes, including to motivate students to be more physically active, to assess students' fitness, and because it is easy and is a traditional component of PE.
- Fitness testing often occurs in a single lesson, disconnected from broader fitness education programmes and with unclear educative aims.
- While some students enjoy fitness testing, the practice can have a negative effect on some students.
- In rethinking 'health' in PE, we suggest moving beyond describing 'what the body is' and instead focussing on what the multiple dimensions of the body can do.
- We recommend embedding testing within a broader fitness education curriculum/unit, enabling students to make decisions that impact their experiences of fitness testing and education, and not publicising the results.

Box 3.4 Next Steps

Based on the content of this chapter and with respect to fitness testing, do the following:

1 Create a fitness education unit, with clear learning intentions and comprising five to ten lessons, that responds to some of the debates shared in this chapter.
2 Within your unit and drawing on various fitness-related activities, include one lesson that addresses each of the dimensions of the body (Cultural, Social, Learning, Physical, Psychological). Be sure to integrate the reflective body across all of these lessons.
3 Consider the ways in which your lessons can 'expand' what the learner's body can do in PE.

References

Alfrey L., Cale L., & Webb, L. (2012). Physical education teachers' continuing professional development in health-related exercise. *Physical Education and Sport Pedagogy*, 17, 477–491.

Alfrey, L., & Gard, M. (2014). A crack where the light gets in: A study of health and physical education teachers' perspectives on fitness testing as a context for learning about health. *Asia–Pacific Journal of Health, Sport and Physical Education*, 5(1), 3–18.

Cale, L., & Harris, J. (2009). Fitness testing in physical education – A misdirected effort in promoting healthy lifestyles and physical activity? *Physical Education and Sport Pedagogy*, 14(1), 89–108.

Fox, N.J. (2012). *The Body*. Cambridge: Polity Press.

Freedson, P., Cureton, K., & Heath, G.W. (2000). Status of field-based fitness testing in children and youth. *Preventive Medicine*, 31(2), 77–85.

Garrett, R., & Wrench, A. (2008). Fitness testing: The pleasure and pain of it. *Healthy Lifestyles Journal*, 55(4), 17–22.

Hopple, C., & Graham, G. (1995). What children think, feel, and know about physical fitness testing. *Journal of Teaching in Physical Education*, 14, 408–417.

Keating, X.D., & Silverman, S. (2004). Teachers' use of fitness tests in school-based physical education programmes. *Measurement in Physical Education and Exercise Science*, 8(3), 145–165.

Kirk, D. (1998). *Schooling Bodies: School Practice and Public Discourse 1880–1950*. London: Leicester University Press.

Ladwig, M., Vazou, S., & Ekkekakis, P. (2018). "My best memory is when I was done with it": PE memories are associated with adult sedentary behavior. *Translational Journal of the ACSM*, 3(16), 119–129.

Landi, D. (2019). *LGBTQ Youth in Physical Education and Sexuality Education: Affect, Curriculum, and (New) Materialism*. Doctoral Thesis. The University of Auckland.

Lodewyk, K.R., & Sullivan, P. (2016). Associations between anxiety, self-efficacy, and outcomes by gender and body size dissatisfaction during fitness in high school physical education. *Physical Education and Sport Pedagogy*, 21(6), 603–615.

McKenzie, T.L., & Lounsbery, M.A. (2009). School physical education: The pill not taken. *American Journal of Lifestyle Medicine*, 3(3), 219–225.

O'Keeffe, B., MacDonncha, C., & Donnelly, A.E. (2021). Students' attitudes towards and experiences of the Youth-fit health-related fitness test battery. *European Physical Education Review*, 27(1), 41–56.

Placek, J.H., Griffin, L.L, Dodds, P., Raymond, C., Tremino, F., & James, A. (2001). Middle school students' conceptions of fitness: The long road to a healthy lifestyle. *Journal of Teaching in Physical Education*, 20, 314–323.

Public Health England. (2013). *National Child Measurement Programme*. https://www.gov.uk/government/collections/national-child-measurement-programme.

Simonton, K.L., Mercier, K., & Garn, A.C. (2019). Do fitness test performances predict students' attitudes and emotions toward physical education? *Physical Education and Sport Pedagogy*, 24(6), 549–564.

Tinning, R. (1985). Physical Education and the cult of slenderness. *ACHPER National Journal*, 107, 10–13.

Tucker, H.J., Bebeley, S.J., & Conteh, M. (2017). Motor skill level of children and adolescents' motivation in physical activity: A major concern for public health and physical education. *International Journal of Science and Research*, 6(12), 482–486.

Vazou, S., Mischo, A., Ladwig, M.A., Ekkekakis, P., & Welk G. (2019). Psychologically informed physical fitness practice in schools: A field experiment. *Psychology of Sport and Exercise*, 40, 143–151.

Willee, A.W. (1973). *Australian Youth Fitness Survey 1971*. Canberra: Australian Government Publishing Service.

Zhu, X., Davis, S., Kirk, N., Haegele, J., & Knott, S. (2018). Inappropriate practices in fitness testing and reporting: Alternative strategies. *Journal of Physical Education, Recreation and Dance*, 89(3), 46–51.

Note

1 Elena is a participant from Landi's (2019) study examining LGBTQIA+ experiences in health, physical activity and educational settings.

4 An Introduction to New PE-for-Health Pedagogies, Approaches and Models

Paul Sammon, Mark Bowler and Ash Casey

Introduction

This chapter examines what we might describe as new PE-for-health pedagogies, approaches or models, which aim to support the promotion of health and physical activity in schools. We begin by highlighting some longstanding concerns around the promotion of health and physical activity in schools and provide a rationale for alternative practice. Next, we explore a number of promising whole-school approaches, before focussing on Models-based Practice (MbP) and presenting a Health-based PE (referred to hereon as HbPE) pedagogical model as an evidence-informed, flexible framework to support the teaching of health-related PE. The chapter concludes with a summary of the main issues and debates raised and some recommendations for practice. Readers are encouraged to reflect on their current philosophy and practice, and to consider how they may draw on some of the features/principles embedded in these new/alternative approaches.

After reading this chapter, you will be able to:

i   explain why there is a need for new 'PE-for-Health' pedagogies;
ii identify and critique some recent whole-school and PE-specific approaches;
iii reflect on your own and/or your school's current teaching of health in PE and promotion of physical activity;
iv plan to implement new 'PE-for-Health' pedagogies in practice.

A Rationale for New PE-for-Health Pedagogies

Promoting lifelong participation in physical activity is viewed as a key goal of PE (United Nations Educational, Scientific and Cultural Organization, 2015), with calls for physical educators to effectively

DOI: 10.4324/9781003225904-4

prepare their students to lead active lifestyles (Harris, 2020). However, evidence indicates that PE has remained largely unsuccessful in achieving this goal (Armour & Harris, 2013; Cale, Harris & Duncombe, 2016; Haerens et al., 2011). While acknowledging the challenges associated with an activity promotion goal, including the relatively low status and limited curriculum time afforded to PE, we argue that the subject has not necessarily always done what is best in the name of health-related learning, with historical issues such as poor teacher preparation and some questionable practice still evident (see Chapters 1 and 3 for a discussion of these).

The teaching of health in PE, as with many areas of the curriculum, is heavily influenced by teachers' beliefs and understanding. For example, although many physical educators embrace a philosophy centred on the promotion of healthy active lifestyles, Harris and Leggett (2015) highlighted a mismatch between some teachers' philosophies and their actual practice. Evidence also reveals a lack of prior experience of health (outside of their own school experiences), limited professional learning opportunities and subsequent gaps in teachers' health-related subject knowledge (Alfrey, Cale & Webb, 2012; Cale, Harris & Duncombe, 2016; Harris, 2020) (see Chapter 1). This suggests that health and physical activity aspirations are unlikely to be realised if physical educators lack the necessary knowledge and skills to effectively teach their students.

Furthermore, teachers' beliefs and understandings, coupled with the dominance of competitive sports in PE, means that the curriculum is typically primarily devoted to games, with little time for specific health-related learning. To compound matters, activities such as fitness testing are widely adopted in the name of health-related PE (Alfrey & Gard, 2014). In attempting to explain the prevalence of fitness testing in many school PE programmes, Cale, Harris and Chen (2014) point to factors such as teacher familiarity with the practice and the relative ease of implementation. Moreover, a fitness testing culture appears to be a 'passed down' tradition in PE, despite long standing concerns with respect to the purpose, validity and reliability of testing children, and questions about its value and appropriateness in the curriculum (Harris, 2020). Indeed, it is argued that the practice of fitness testing, such as compelling students to perform tests in front of their peers and comparing scores, is likely to be a negative experience for many young people, particularly the most vulnerable, which may lead them to ultimately disengage from physical activity (Harris & Cale, 2019). See Chapter 3 for a more detailed insight into and critique of fitness testing as a debated and contested health-related practice.

Despite the implementation of numerous health-based intervention programmes in PE, Haerens et al. (2011) suggested that these have largely failed to stimulate sustained pedagogical change in teachers' practice. Furthermore, there is little evidence that they have been successful in increasing student physical activity participation. In light of this, we next discuss the potential of some whole-school approaches for health and physical activity promotion, before shifting our focus specifically to health-related learning in PE.

Box 4.1 Health-Related Learning in PE

Reflect on your health-related PE experience and consider the following questions:

1   To what extent is health-related learning valued in your PE programme?
2   What is the philosophy behind your health-related PE curriculum?
3   Can you identify any gaps in your health-related subject knowledge?

Whole-School Approaches for Health and Physical Activity Promotion

The design and implementation of multi-component, whole-school approaches to health and physical activity promotion have increasingly been viewed as a global priority (World Health Organization, 2018). Based largely on the socio-ecological model, whole-school approaches recognise the need to move beyond the curriculum to help address the multiple influences on young people's physical activity behaviour. There are several potential benefits of whole-school approaches, such as fostering a positive culture towards physical activity and encouraging a shared responsibility in its promotion across the school community (staff, students, parents/guardians). However, Webster et al. (2015) warn that there is unlikely to be one approach which can be applied with consistent success in different contexts. Furthermore, it is still unclear what the most effective whole-school approaches for sustained change in physical activity behaviour are and how they can be successfully employed (Daly-Smith et al., 2020).

Comprehensive School Physical Activity Programs

One well established whole-school approach, Comprehensive School Physical Activity Programs (CSPAP), involves a multi-component framework where schools explore a range of potential opportunities for their students to develop the knowledge, skills, and confidence necessary for lifelong physical activity participation (Centers for Disease Control and Prevention [CDC], 2013). As illustrated in Figure 4.1, a CSPAP includes five recognised components: (1) quality PE; (2) physical activity during the school day; (3) physical activity before and after school; (4) staff engagement and (5) family and community involvement.

The implementation and sustainability of a successful CSPAP requires careful coordination and planning. Consequently, a series of steps are suggested (see CDC, 2013), such as initially electing a Physical Activity Leader, auditing existing physical activity opportunities, and creating a vision statement for the CSPAP. Considering some of these steps in more detail, it is anticipated that the Physical Activity Leader would most likely be a PE teacher, although evidence highlights that some physical educators may lack the specialist knowledge and skills required to assume this leadership role (Armour & Harris, 2013; Armour et al., 2015; Daly-Smith et al., 2020). Alternatively, the Physical Activity Leader could be another member of school staff, such as a head teacher or a pastoral lead. When auditing existing physical activity provision, it is important to note where and when students have opportunities to be active during the school day and what types of activities are most effective in increasing students' activity levels.

Quality PE is recognised as the core component of an effective CSPAP, as it is arguably the key context in schools where children and young people should develop the knowledge, skills and attitudes to be active. According to the CDC (2013), quality PE should be fully

Figure 4.1 Framework for Comprehensive School Physical Activity Program (adapted from Carson & Webster, 2020)

inclusive and provide an enjoyable experience for all students. In addition, it is recommended that students are active for the majority of PE lesson time in a variety of meaningful contexts and that they are taught how to adopt active lifestyles. For example, teachers should embed health-related knowledge across their PE programmes, such as signposting where students can safely be active out of class, both during the school day and in their local community. Once schools have established quality PE as a core component of their CSPAP, the next step should be to focus on implementing one other component well, for instance, promoting physical activity during the school day, rather than trying to implement all remaining components simultaneously.

Health Optimizing PE

Another whole-school approach that links closely with CSPAP is Health Optimizing PE (HOPE) (Metzler et al., 2013a, 2013b). Fundamental to HOPE is the belief that teaching and learning about health takes place in a variety of contexts. Metzler et al. (2013a) stress that HOPE should be viewed as a comprehensive and sustainable whole-school physical activity programme and not a model which is solely implemented during PE curriculum time. The primary aim of HOPE is to support young people to gain the necessary knowledge and skills for lifelong physical activity participation. A HOPE programme comprises eight strands for physical activity promotion across different contexts (Table 4.1). For example, *Strand 4: Community-Based Physical Activity*, asks teachers to signpost opportunities for children to be active in their local community, while *Strand 7: Physical Activity Literacy*, recommends that teachers support their students to make informed decisions about physical activity in their daily lives (Metzler et al., 2013b).

Metzler and colleagues (2013b, p.34) make three suggestions for starting a HOPE programme:

1   Conduct a school audit to determine existing opportunities for children to be physically active, then identify HOPE strands and set future goals.
2   Slowly build on existing strengths, adding new strands that have a high possibility of success.
3   Explore outside support, such as partnerships with universities, to collaborate on the design and implementation of HOPE programmes.

Table 4.1 HOPE Model Programme Strands (Adapted from Metzler et al., 2013a)

Strand 1	Before and After School Physical Activity
Strand 2	Sport, Dance and Other Movement Forms
Strand 3	Family/Home Education
Strand 4	Community-Based Physical Activity
Strand 5	Health-Related Fitness
Strand 6	Diet and Nutrition for Physical Activity
Strand 7	Physical Activity Literacy
Strand 8	Integration of HOPE across other Subjects

To illustrate this process, teachers could begin a HOPE programme by identifying one or two areas following a school audit of physical activity opportunities (such as the two strands mentioned earlier). New strands can then be added gradually over time together with exploring outside support opportunities. Teachers should have autonomy and flexibility to develop their own version of HOPE (i.e. strands, learning activities and assessment opportunities) suitable for their specific contexts, yet they must adhere to the model's primary aim of supporting young people to gain the necessary knowledge and skills for lifelong physical activity participation.

Creating Active Schools

Recently, there have been similar developments to CSPAP and HOPE in the United Kingdom (UK) to support whole-school approaches to health and physical activity promotion. The Creating Active Schools (CAS) framework (Daly-Smith et al., 2020) stresses the importance of embedding physical activity at the heart of school life. Establishing a school-wide ethos for activity promotion is seen to be essential in providing quality experiences for all young people and, subsequently, for sustained behaviour change to occur (Daly-Smith et al., 2020). Specifically, CAS aims to support schools to increase their students' daily physical activity, working towards achieving a minimum of 30 minutes of in-school and 60 minutes of total activity across the day, in line with national guidelines for children and young people in the UK (Chief Medical Officers, 2019). Co-production is at the heart of a CAS approach, with schools encouraged to be centrally involved in designing bespoke physical activity programmes to reflect their specific contexts.

The CAS framework was initially designed to identify the multiple components needed to facilitate whole-school physical activity implementation (Daly-Smith et al., 2020). Five groups of people were highlighted as key stakeholders: school leaders; teachers and other school staff; children/young people; parents/guardians and wider stakeholders (e.g. active school coordinators). School leaders are expected to drive the vision and policy, teachers and other school staff to deliver activity initiatives, while children/young people may be provided with opportunities to lead activities during the school day.

Together with these five key stakeholder groups, seven opportunities or contexts for influencing physical activity were identified: (1) curricular lessons (other than PE); (2) PE lessons; (3) break/lunchtimes (recess); (4) trips and events, such as sports days; (5) before/after school clubs; (6) active travel and (7) family/community physical activity out of school (Daly-Smith et al., 2020). Of these opportunities, embedding active learning in curricular lessons (other than PE) is viewed as having the greatest potential impact on increasing physical activity, as this is typically where students are most sedentary during the school day. However, PE lessons are also highlighted as an important context to positively influence young people's physical activity behaviour. This suggests that all teachers should be supported in how to implement practical behaviour change strategies and become effective whole-school physical activity practitioners.

Promoting Active Lifestyles Project

A second development in the UK is the Promoting Active Lifestyles (PAL) Project (Harris, Cale & Hooper, 2020a), which was established to help physical educators to create and implement approaches to promoting active lifestyles among young people. As Chapter 6 specifically focusses on the PAL Project, our purpose here is to provide a brief overview. PAL involved the co-construction of 20 principles associated with the promotion of active lifestyles, with 10 principles categorised as whole-school and 10 as PE-specific. Example whole-school principles include: (1) teaching the physical activity for health guidelines during Personal, Social and Health Education; (2) highlighting the importance of active lifestyles across the school community (i.e. all staff, students, governors and parents/carers) and (3) promoting active travel to and from school (e.g. walking, cycling, scooting). In contrast, PE-specific principles include: (1) teaching students the broad range of benefits (physical, psychological and social) of adopting an active lifestyle; (2) regularly highlighting where students can be active in their local community and (3) identifying low active students and offering them (and their parents/carers) bespoke activity opportunities (Harris, Cale & Hooper, 2020b).

When adopting PAL principles, it is recommended that teachers begin with those which are most relevant to their specific context and then apply further principles once the preliminary ones have been established in practice. The initial outcomes from the PAL Project are encouraging, with teachers reporting that their involvement altered their thinking and subsequent teaching about active lifestyles. Harris, Cale and Hooper (2020b) proposed that this principle-based approach to pedagogical change demonstrates a positive response to calls for evidence-based PE-for-health pedagogies, which can support teachers in becoming more effective champions of physical activity.

Box 4.2 Promoting Health and Physical Activity across the Whole School

Reflect on the promotion of health and physical activity in your school and consider the following questions:

1 Can you provide examples of how you promote health and physical activity across your school?
2 Who is responsible for coordinating your whole-school approach and what professional development have they had in this area?
3 How might you incorporate some of the ideas and approaches presented to enhance physical activity opportunities across your school community?

In addition to whole-school approaches for health and physical activity promotion, there have been calls for employing Models-based Practice (MbP) in PE and the development of a specific Health-based PE pedagogical model (Haerens et al., 2011).

A Pedagogical Model for Health-Based PE

The multi-activity approach (MAA) has been recognised as the dominant model used in PE worldwide (Kirk, 2010). Typically, this is a sport-focussed approach which involves prioritising the teaching of activity content and developing students' technical skills across short units of learning. The dominance of MAA endures, despite strong reservations regarding its inclusivity and, of relevance here, its suitability in achieving health-related outcomes (Armour & Harris, 2013). In seeking an alternative approach to curriculum design in PE, Casey and Kirk (2021) have proposed MbP. They suggest that such an approach allows teachers to re-consider what pedagogy (i.e. curriculum, teaching, learning and assessment) means to them in their context, and choose different pedagogical models around which to build a new curriculum. Positioned as the organising centre of MbP, Casey and Kirk (2021) argue that using a pedagogical model shifts the focus from activity (e.g. fitness testing) to learning (e.g. about healthy, active lifestyles) which, in turn, helps teachers better achieve the learning aspirations they have for their students.

Recognising the need for an evidence-informed framework to specifically support the teaching of health-related PE, Haerens et al. (2011) proposed the development of a HbPE pedagogical model. As HbPE is the specific focus of Chapter 5, we provide just an overview of the model and some examples of how it might translate in practice here. With 'valuing a physically active life' positioned as HbPE's main idea, Haerens and colleagues argued that this would only be achieved if individuals were intrinsically motivated to engage in physical activity. Bowler and Sammon (2020, p. 61) further explained that teaching for valuing involves 'helping individuals to see the intrinsic benefits of physical activity and securing meaningful experiences through their PE journey'. Four learning aspirations were also highlighted by Bowler and Sammon (2020) to help realise the main idea of 'valuing a physically active life'. These four aspirations (see Table 4.2) aim to support all young people to become habitual, informed, motivated and critical movers.

To maximise the achievement of a model's learning aspirations, Casey and Kirk (2021) advocate the design of specific critical elements to guide teacher and student behaviour. In designing HbPE, Sammon and Bowler (2020) proposed four critical elements which reflect both the main idea and the learning aspirations of the model: (1) the teacher promotes meaningful physical activity; (2) the teacher supports students to be informed movers; (3) the teacher creates a needs-supportive learning environment and (4) the teacher encourages students to become critical movers. For example, teachers should promote physical activity by teaching students how to identify and meet personal activity targets. Alternatively, the learning aspiration that students will

Table 4.2 HBPE Learning Aspirations (Adapted from Bowler and Sammon, 2020)

Students who 'value a physically active life' will:

---

1 Lead an active lifestyle through regular participation in meaningful physical activity **(habitual mover)**
2 Demonstrate a positive attitude and perceived competence in chosen physical activities through high levels of effort and individual challenge **(motivated mover)**
3 Explain how and where to engage in physical activities of personal interest, the effects of an active lifestyle, and how to participate safely and effectively to achieve their personal goals **(informed mover)**
4 Evaluate socio-cultural barriers to physical activity involvement and become activists (movement promoters) to positively affect their own and others' physical activity environment **(critical mover)**

---

become informed movers requires them to develop knowledge and understanding in relation to how and where they can be physically active in their local community.

When planning learning intentions, Sammon and Bowler (2020) advised teachers to begin by working back from both the main idea (i.e. valuing) and the key learning aspirations (i.e. movers) of HbPE. Thus, some examples of learning intentions for students may include: (1) identify how to be active in their local community, (2) demonstrate engagement with their personal physical activity pledges and (3) recognise common barriers to participation and how to overcome them. In terms of assessing students' learning during HbPE, it is recommended that teachers prioritise the affective domain, but there should also be opportunities for learning through the cognitive, physical and social domains respectively (Haerens et al., 2011; Sammon & Bowler, 2020). Consequently, assessment may focus on students' personal behaviours, such as their enthusiasm and motivation for being physically active, or on the extent to which they support others to be active.

HbPE, like other pedagogical models, has what Casey and Kirk (2021) term, 'space for manoeuvre' in response to local contextual requirements. For example, due to timetabling or facility constraints, teachers may plan and implement modified HbPE programmes in terms of the duration, learning activities and the assessment strategies employed. However, the main idea (i.e. valuing), the learning aspirations (i.e. becoming movers) and the critical elements of the model should not be modified.

Box 4.3 Employing the HbPE Model in Practice

Having read about HbPE, now reflect on the model and consider the following questions:

1   Do you encourage all students to value and lead active lifestyles?
2   What teaching skills will be required to support students to achieve the learning aspirations/goals of HbPE?
3   How might you employ HbPE in your curriculum and what further support will you require to effectively implement, and sustain, this model in practice?

Conclusion

This chapter has introduced some new PE-for-health pedagogies, approaches and models. Initially, we highlighted some longstanding concerns around the promotion of health and physical activity in schools and provided a rationale for alternative practice. We explored a number of promising whole-school approaches such as CSPAP, HOPE, CAS and PAL and illustrated how they might be successfully planned and implemented in practice. Next, we discussed employing MbP and pedagogical models, notably HbPE, as a framework to support the teaching of health-related PE and we provided some insight into the main idea, learning aspirations and critical features of the model. The chapter concludes with a summary of the main issues and debates raised and some recommendations for practice.

Summary and Recommendations

- Promoting lifelong participation in physical activity is a key goal of PE, yet the subject is struggling to achieve this goal due to historical issues such as poor teacher preparation and questionable practice.
- Whole-school, multi-component approaches to health and physical activity promotion are increasingly viewed as a global priority to help address the many influences on young people's activity behaviour.
- CSPAP aspire to develop young people's knowledge, skills and confidence for lifelong physical activity, with quality PE a core

component, and successful implementation involving a series of steps such as electing a Physical Activity Leader, auditing existing physical activity opportunities and creating a vision statement.
- The primary aim of HOPE is to support young people's participation in physical activity, with teachers having autonomy and flexibility to develop their own programmes suitable for their specific contexts.
- CAS recommends the establishment of a school-wide activity promotion ethos for sustained behaviour change to occur, with embedding physical activity in curricular lessons (other than PE) viewed as critically important.
- PAL is a whole-school approach which supported teachers to co-construct and implement a novel set of principles to promote active lifestyles, both across the school community and in PE.
- MbP provides an alternative, evidence-informed and flexible approach to the traditional MAA curriculum design in PE and shifts the focus from activity (e.g. fitness testing) to learning (e.g. about healthy, active lifestyles).
- The HbPE model, with 'valuing a physically active life' as its main idea, aims to support all young people to become habitual, motivated, informed and critical movers. When implementing HbPE, teachers should employ the four critical elements and prioritise the affective domain, but there is 'space for manoeuvre' in response to local contextual requirements.

Bibliography

Armour, K., & Harris, J. (2013). Making the case for developing new PE-for-health pedagogies. *Quest*, 65, 201–219.

Carson, R.L., & Webster, C.A. (2020). *Comprehensive School Physical Activity Programs: Putting Research into Evidence-Based Practice*. Champaign, IL: Human Kinetics.

Daly-Smith, A., Quarmby, T., Archbold, V.S.J. et al. (2020). Using a multi-stakeholder experience-based design process to co-develop the Creating Active Schools Framework. *International Journal of Behavioral Nutrition and Physical Act*ivity, 17, 13. https://doi.org/10.1186/s12966-020-0917-z

References

Alfrey, L., Cale, L., & Webb, L. (2012). Physical education teachers' continuing professional development in health-related exercise. *Physical Education and Sport Pedagogy*, 17(5), 477–491.

Alfrey, L., & Gard, M. (2014). A crack where the light gets in: A study of health and physical education teachers' perspectives on fitness testing as a context for learning about health. *Asia–Pacific Journal of Health, Sport and Physical Education*, 5(1), 3–18.

Armour, K., & Harris, J. (2013). Making the case for developing new PE-for-Health pedagogies. *Quest*, 65(2), 201–219.

Armour, K., Quennerstedt, M., Chambers, F., & Makopoulou, K. (2015). What is 'effective' CPD for contemporary physical education teachers? A Deweyan framework. *Sport Education and Society*, 22(7), 799–811.

Bowler, M., & Sammon, P. (2020). Health-based physical education – A framework for promoting active lifestyles in children and young people. Part 1: Introducing a new pedagogical model for health-based physical education. *Physical Education Matters*, 15(3), 60–63.

Cale, L., Harris, J., & Chen, M.H. (2014). Monitoring health, activity and fitness in physical education: Its current and future state of health. *Sport, Education and Society*, 19(4), 376–397.

Cale, L., Harris, J., & Duncombe, R. (2016). Promoting physical activity in secondary schools: Growing expectations, same old issues? *European Physical Education Review*, 22(4), 526–544.

Carson, R.L., & Webster, C.A. (2020). *Comprehensive School Physical Activity Programs: Putting Research into Evidence-Based Practice*. Champaign, IL: Human Kinetics.

Casey, A., & Kirk, D. (2021). *Models-Based Practice in Physical Education*. London: Routledge.

Centers for Disease Control and Prevention. (2013). *Comprehensive School Physical Activity Programs: A Guide for Schools*. Atlanta, GA: U.S. Department of Health and Human Services. Available at: https://www.cdc.gov/healthyschools/physicalactivity/pdf/13_242620-A_CSPAP_SchoolPhysActivityPrograms_Final_508_12192013.pdf (Accessed 19 November 2021).

Chief Medical Officers. (2019). *UK Chief Medical Officers' Physical Activity Guidelines*. Available at: https://www.gov.uk/government/publications/-physical-activity-guidelines-uk-chief-medical-officers-report (Accessed 22 November 2021).

Daly-Smith, A., Quarmby, T., Archbold, V.S.J. et al. (2020). Using a multi-stakeholder experience-based design process to co-develop the Creating Active Schools Framework. *International Journal of Behavioral Nutrition and Physical Activity*, 17, 13. https://doi.org/10.1186/s12966-020-0917-z

Haerens, L., Kirk, D., Cardon, G., & De Bourdeaudhuij, I. (2011). Toward the development of a pedagogical model for health-based physical education. *Quest*, 63, 321–338.

Harris, J. (2020). *Association for Physical Education Health Position Paper*. Available at: https://www.afpe.org.uk/afpe-2020-health-position-paper/ (Accessed 1 July 2021).

Harris, J., & Cale, L. (2019). *Promoting Active Lifestyles in Schools*. Champaign, IL: Human Kinetics.

Harris, J., Cale, L., & Hooper, O. (2020a). The Promoting Active Lifestyles (PAL) Project: A principle-based approach to pedagogical change. *The Curriculum Journal*, 32(1), 87–102.

Harris, J., Cale, L., & Hooper, O. (2020b). Prompting pedagogical change through promoting active lifestyles paradoxes. *International Journal of Environmental Research and Public Health*, 17(21), 65–79.

Harris, J., & Leggett, G. (2015). Influences on the expression of health within PE curricula in secondary schools in England and Wales. *Sport, Education and Society*, 20(7), 908–923.

Kirk, D. (2010) *Physical Education Futures*. London: Routledge.

Metzler, M., McKenzie, T., Van der Mars, H., Barrett-Williams, S., & Ellis, R. (2013a). Health Optimizing Physical Education (HOPE): A new curriculum for school programs. Part 1: Establishing the need and describing the Model. *Journal of Physical Education, Recreation & Dance*, 84(4), 41–47.

Metzler, M., McKenzie, T., Van der Mars, H., Barrett-Williams, S., & Ellis, R. (2013b). Health Optimizing Physical Education (HOPE): A new curriculum for school programs. Part 2: Teacher knowledge and collaboration. *Journal of Physical Education, Recreation & Dance*, 84(5), 25–34.

Sammon, P., & Bowler, M. (2020). Health-based physical education – A framework for promoting active lifestyles in children and young people. Part 2: Health-based physical education in practice. *Physical Education Matters*, 15(3), 64–66.

United Nations Educational, Scientific and Cultural Organization. (2015). *Quality PE: Guidelines for Policy-Makers*. UNESCO Publishing.

Webster, C.A., Beets, M., Weaver, R.G., Vazou, S., & Russ, L. (2015). Rethinking recommendations for implementing comprehensive school physical activity programs: A partnership model. *Quest*, 67(2), 185–202.

World Health Organization. (2018). *Global Standards and Health Promoting Schools*. Geneva, Switzerland: World Health Organization.

5 Health-Based Physical Education

A Pedagogical Model in Focus

Mark Bowler, Paul Sammon and Ash Casey

Introduction

As previous chapters have argued, approaches internationally for teaching health-related PE have largely been ineffective in supporting young people to lead healthy, active lifestyles. This chapter provides a rationale and framework for the Health-based Physical Education pedagogical model (referred to throughout this chapter as HbPE) which reconceptualises the way in which health-related PE might be taught and experienced. The chapter explains why a pedagogical model for HbPE is needed, provides a background to its development and then explores what Casey and Kirk (2021) term the main idea, learning aspirations, critical elements and pedagogy underpinning the model. Readers are supported to review the HbPE framework to consider how to translate this to their own school contexts.

After reading this chapter, you will be able to:

i   explain why a pedagogical model for HbPE might support effective practice in PE;
ii   identify the background and development of HbPE;
iii describe HbPE's framework i.e. the 'main idea', 'critical elements', 'learning aspirations' and 'pedagogy';
iv   explore opportunities to implement HbPE in your PE curriculum to support students to value a physically active life.

Why a Pedagogical Model for Health-Based PE?

A number of health-related PE practices have been critiqued for their emphasis on fitness, exercise and sport content (see Chapter 3 which focusses on fitness testing as a debated and contested PE-for-health practice). In many cases, there is also a mismatch between teachers' well-meaning philosophies (usually a 'fitness for life' goal, or similar) and

DOI: 10.4324/9781003225904-5

their practice (which tends to focus on 'fitness for sport/performance') (Harris & Leggett, 2015). Consequently, there are missed opportunities to focus on a much more impactful outcome for young people in PE and to place a greater emphasis on 'physical activity as a resource for life' (Bowler, 2019). HbPE, in seeking improved health outcomes in young people, supports teachers to raise the profile of adopting active lifestyles, for which there is convincing evidence of physical, social, emotional, personal and cognitive benefits. This is even more important in current times given that globally around 80% of adolescents are insufficiently active for health purposes (Guthold et al., 2020).

Pedagogical models are positioned by Casey and Kirk (2021) as the organising centre for designing curricula, replacing 'sports' to achieve a richer variety of subject goals. Models are design specifications to support teachers in developing local programmes in their contexts and, while their frameworks are comprehensive, they offer teachers much flexibility in their implementation. Pedagogical models exist for the teaching and learning of foci such as cooperation, games, personal and social responsibility and fitness and health (McConnell, 2015; Metzler et al., 2013). However, these models have diverse goals designed to meet the broad aims of PE, and arguably do not emphasise the unique aspiration of prioritising physical activity for life that HbPE presents. Yet, the need for such a model has been recognised (Armour & Harris, 2013; Fernandez-Rio, 2016). Given the ineffectiveness of previous approaches to health-related PE and the articulated importance of supporting young people to lead healthy, active lifestyles in PE curricula around the world, the potential for a pedagogical model with valuing physical activity as its main idea is significant. Some might argue that such a model is vital if we are going to support more effective PE-for-health pedagogies (Armour & Harris, 2013).

Box 5.1 Health- or Physical Activity Learning in PE Programmes

Consider the following questions in relation to the aims and subject matter of your PE programme:

1 Do explicit health- or physical activity-related learning aims feature in your PE programme?
2 If so, how well do these aims align with the subject matter and activities of your PE units of learning?

The Development of Health-Based PE

HbPE was a key outcome of Mark and Paul's PhD studies between 2011 and 2019. The focus of this doctoral research[1] evolved from the publication of 'Toward the development of a pedagogical model for health-based physical education' (Haerens et al., 2011). The primary aim of Mark's PhD (Bowler, 2019) was to develop a comprehensive, evidence-informed HbPE pedagogical model. A secondary aim was to support teachers in the design, implementation and evaluation of programmes using the HbPE model in their schools. The study employed participatory action research in 2 schools, with a total of 9 teachers and 263 students aged 11–14 years. Paul's PhD explored the same teachers' learning experiences during a collaborative and sustained professional development programme centred on the HbPE model (Sammon, 2019). The content and ideas presented in this chapter stem largely from these two doctoral studies and our subsequent collaborations.

HbPE was initially developed through an eight-stage process between 2011 and 2019. This included extensive reviews of literature, drafting a conceptual framework, piloting key features of this and then co-constructing PE programmes with teachers, followed by implementing and revising the programmes. On completion of the school-based HbPE programmes, feedback from an international audience of PE and sport pedagogy professionals led to further refinement of the model. While the 'prototype' HbPE pedagogical model framework (stage 8) was presented in Mark's PhD thesis, it has since been developed, with the modifications published first in 2020 (Bowler & Sammon, 2020; Sammon & Bowler, 2020) and now in this chapter. The key development in this book represents the adoption of new terminology proposed by Casey and Kirk (2021), i.e. the 'main idea', 'critical elements', 'learning aspirations' and 'pedagogy' for the model.

Health-Based PE: The Pedagogical Model Framework

Main Idea

The main idea of HbPE, 'valuing a physically active life', stems from the work of Siedentop (1996). Siedentop associated valuing with three crucial qualities: (1) participation – people organise their lives so that they can be active regularly, (2) literate participants – are knowledgeable in their chosen physical activities and use this knowledge to maintain and enhance the practice of their pursuit and (3) critical participants – who understand barriers to physical activity participation and work to find solutions for their own and others' involvement. Valuing movement is also closely aligned with the notions of meaningfulness and intrinsic motivation, which are fundamental characteristics that support a commitment to physical activity participation (Fletcher et al., 2021; Teixeira et al., 2012).

Fletcher et al. (2021) have presented a framework to support meaningful experiences for young people in PE. In relation to health-related PE, a meaningful curriculum will prioritise the students' experience in PE above 'a narrow set of utilitarian, health-based outcomes for young people where disease prevention through personal fitness is privileged over seeking the joy of movement' (Fletcher et al., 2021, p. 5). As Kretchmar proposed, 'one of the greatest things about physical activity and play is that they [can] make our lives go better, not just longer' (2006, p. 6 [emphasis added]).

Six key features of meaningful PE have been identified as important for practitioners to promote in and through their teaching (Fletcher et al., 2021). These are social interaction, challenge, fun, motor competence, personally relevant learning and delight. We argue that these features, in supporting meaningful PE experiences for young people, can also help them to value physical activity. Building on the notion of 'valuing a physically active life' and considering the priorities of meaningful PE, a fuller definition of the main idea for HbPE is:

> Valuing a physically active life, so that students learn to value and practise physical activity for their health and wellbeing, joy, social interaction, challenge, competence, and personally relevant learning experiences.
>
> (Bowler, 2019, p. 212)

Box 5.2 The Main Idea of HbPE

Reflecting on the main idea of HbPE:

1   Consider how well your students evidence the three qualities of 'valuing a physically active life' (participation, literate and critical).
2   Discuss with your colleagues the extent to which the six key features of 'meaningful PE' (social interaction, challenge, fun, motor competence, personally relevant learning and delight) feature within your PE curriculum.

Learning Aspirations

To achieve the main idea of 'valuing a physically active life', four learning aspirations have been developed. While these are not hierarchical, we feel it is crucial to emphasise the importance of physical activity participation as an overall goal for HbPE. This is reflected in the adoption of the term 'mover' in each aspiration – a term coined by Hastie (2010) to describe an individual who is regularly physically active in a range of unstructured and/or structured physical activities. The learning aspirations for HbPE are therefore to support the development of *habitual movers, motivated movers, informed movers* and *critical movers*.

Habitual mover: Supporting young people to be *habitual movers* is a central aspiration for HbPE because individuals who value physical activity will most easily demonstrate this in their participation habits (Siedentop, 1996). A key goal here is to support students to participate in physical activity for the wide range of reasons and benefits that will enrich their lives (Bailey et al., 2013). Supporting students to work towards achieving the physical activity guidelines for young people or, if these are met, towards other agreed goals is important. These might include more moderate to vigorous physical activity, up to several hours of physical activity per day, increasing the number of instances of vigorous activity or reducing sedentary time. Equally, goals might relate to wider health-related outcomes such as improved endurance, strength, flexibility or wellbeing. It should be noted that the social relationships developed in activity settings are the key to realising the wider benefits of physical activity, and teachers should therefore support students to set goals which emphasise personally relevant experiences and not merely improved health outcomes.

Motivated mover: The underlying theories of HbPE include self-determination theory, the social ecological model of health and correlates of physical activity (see Bowler, 2019). While an explanation of these theories is beyond the scope of this chapter, it is worth noting here the importance of autonomous or intrinsic forms of motivation for a *motivated mover* to sustain their physical activity participation. While intrinsic motivation is a key aspiration in HbPE, the wide range of motives for participation serve as a prompt for teachers to work with their students as individuals to help them to establish their own motives and preferences for taking part in physical activity, such as being active with friends, finding a personal challenge, or increasing their daily steps. Perceived competence is also an important motive for many individuals' continued participation in physical activity (Biddle et al., 2021). Therefore, approaches that support students to participate effectively and efficiently in different types of activity contexts to develop their physical competence is a further key factor for teachers to consider in relation to motivation.

Informed mover: The importance of developing participants' knowledge and understanding of physical activity, including of the process of behaviour change, is deemed crucial (Michie, Van Stralen & West, 2011). Consequently, developing *informed movers* is an important aspiration when supporting young people to engage in physically active lifestyles. To support learning through HbPE, there should be a clear focus on how and where to be active in the school and community, the effects of physical activity participation (short and long term) and how to participate safely and effectively in activities for increased physical benefit. With specific reference to the benefits of physical activity, it is vital to recognise the affective and social benefits (e.g. enjoyment, friendships, well-being) of participation, as many young people seem more engaged by these emotional factors (Martins et al., 2015).

Critical mover: Valuing a physically active life is supported when young people can identify barriers to physical activity participation and work to become physical activity advocates for their own and others' benefit. Critical movers might promote physical activity locally, and even regionally, nationally or internationally. However, our work with teachers, supported by literature (e.g. Walton-Fisette, Sutherland & Hill, 2019), suggests that some practitioners need a greater socio-cultural awareness to support their students to develop an appreciation of equity, difference and social justice in physical activity and thereby become critical movers. In developing critical movers, teachers can support young people to become more proactive in facilitating positive physical activity outcomes in commonly marginalised groups, including girls, individuals with special educational needs and disabilities, those of lower socio-economic status and/or who are obese. Thus, teachers may need to help students to develop the skills to advocate and support others to be active and to manage the pressures and wider influences that can serve as barriers to physical activity, such as peers, family, media and wider culture. In this sense, students need to acquire a broad socio-cultural awareness and relevant leadership skills to develop into outstanding critical movers.

Box 5.3 The Learning Aspirations of HbPE

Reflecting on the learning aspirations of HbPE:

1   How well does your health-related PE programme support students to be habitual, motivated, informed and critical movers?
2   Are some of the learning aspirations more or less prevalent in your programme, and consequently which might you afford more attention to in supporting the development of valuing a physically active life?

Critical Elements

The critical elements of a pedagogical model highlight its individual shape and provide users with a sense of what the creators view to be its essential and unique features (Casey & Kirk, 2021). For us, the critical elements of HbPE provide a way for teachers to emphasise the main idea and achieve the learning aspirations. Consequently, the language used in the critical elements aligns closely with these components of HbPE. To support practitioners' use of the model, we created the acronym 'PINC', which corresponds with the key expectations (in italics) of each of the four critical elements: Teacher *promotes* meaningful physical activity; Teacher supports students to be *informed* movers; Teacher creates a *needs-supportive* learning environment and Teacher encourages students to become *critical* movers.

The critical element 'Teacher *promotes* meaningful physical activity' is of central importance, both within and beyond the lesson, given that neither out-of-class physical activity signposting nor high levels of meaningful activity are key features of most PE lessons. In supporting the development of a motivated mover, the teacher should create a *needs-supportive* learning climate (Teixeira et al., 2012), developing student perceptions of autonomy, belonging and competence. Meanwhile, developing *informed* and *critical* movers requires teachers to help students to acquire knowledge and understanding of physical activity and the skills to become movement promoters to others. Examples of strategies to implement each element of 'PINC' can be found in Bowler (2019) and Sammon and Bowler (2020).

Box 5.4 The Critical Features of HbPE

In relation to the critical features of HbPE:
What specific strategies would support the achievement of the four critical elements within and beyond your health-related PE curriculum?

Pedagogy

Pedagogy, which Casey and Kirk (2021) refer to as the interdependence of curriculum, teaching, learning and assessment, is key in the implementation of HbPE. We have framed HbPE as a pedagogical model to teach health-related PE as a central and explicit area of the curriculum, revisited and developed throughout a student's PE journey, with each unit taught for a sustained period (12 weeks or longer). As part of a models-based curriculum, HbPE might be taught alongside other pedagogical models that have their own aspirations and unique features. In addition to explicit units of HbPE, the main idea, learning aspirations and critical elements of the model might inform wider curriculum planning, for example, through making 'valuing physical activity' or 'motivated movers' a priority in PE or across other subject areas (see Chapter 4 for a discussion of whole-school approaches).

HbPE identifies five assumptions of learning and teaching that we believe will help guide teachers in their design and implementation of school-based programmes. The assumptions focus on evidence-informed practices which support the achievement of the main idea, learning aspirations and critical elements.

Assumption 1: Teachers prioritise a physical activity for life (rather than a fitness, sport or performance) approach.

Assumption 2: Changes in physical activity behaviour require extended periods of learning in multiple learning domains (affective, cognitive, physical and social) with the affective domain taking highest priority.

Assumption 3: What is learnt in HbPE programmes must be meaningful and draw from and be transferable into young people's leisure time.

Assumption 4: Approaches must support perceptions of autonomy, competence and relatedness among all students to develop their intrinsic motivation for physical activity.

Assumption 5: HbPE programmes should draw on multiple school, family and community strategies.

Curriculum Design

Physical activity behaviour change is complex and takes time. Lally et al. (2010) suggest that about 66 days of repetition are needed to form a new habit. This is broadly supported by a recent systematic review of research on affective learning in PE which identified that 'it is possible that a minimum length of 8 weeks may be needed to observe significant changes in students' basic psychological need satisfaction and autonomous motivation' (Teraoka et al., 2021, p. 469). These findings align with pedagogical calls for longer units of learning in PE to develop deeper knowledge and higher levels of competence (Kirk, 2010). For this reason, we propose that programmes of HbPE should last for at least one school term (typically 12 weeks), with health-related learning also being reinforced through other aspects of PE and wider school approaches. It should be remembered that HbPE is aligned with one of the fundamental goals of PE (promoting active lifestyles) and should therefore arguably take a 'pivotal' (Fernandez-Rio, 2016, p. 5) position in PE curricula.

As previously reported, the fitness, performance and sport-focussed activities commonly incorporated in health-related PE programmes have been shown to have little impact in supporting young people to lead healthy, active lifestyles. Furthermore, such activities can lead to young people developing negative perceptions of physical activity. This has led to debates on what activities and content should be included in a health-related PE curriculum. Some suggest a balance of activities that students will enjoy both now and as adults (Lund & Tannehill, 2010), and others propose the inclusion of more lifetime or informal activities (O'Connor & Penney, 2021) such as walking, jogging, running, swimming, cycling, resistance exercise and martial arts. A key priority for schools should be to ensure there are suitable activity transfer opportunities between the school and community.

Box 5.5   The Assumptions of HbPE

In relation to the assumptions of HbPE:

1   To what extent does your experience of teaching health-related PE programmes align with the five assumptions of learning and teaching for HbPE?
2   How might you integrate (or further integrate) these assumptions into your programmes?

Teaching and Learning

Our work with teachers has generated a range of strategies that facilitate the successful implementation of HbPE (see Bowler, 2019; Bowler & Sammon, 2020; Sammon & Bowler, 2020). The elements of habitual and motivated movers have been developed using 'physical activity buddies', where students support each other's progress over a sustained period. Teachers have also used in- and post-lesson physical activity challenges to promote higher levels of physical activity engagement, while the use of physical activity diaries has helped students to monitor and set targets for physical activity. Supported by the principles of self-determination theory and meaningful PE, we have also seen the benefits of teaching using approaches that support the needs of autonomy, belonging and competence in students.

To develop informed and critical movers, we have found it important to balance teacher presentation of information with questioning strategies and guided practical activities because HbPE (like health-related PE more broadly) should not be seen as a theoretical area of PE. The use of resources and infographics relating to physical activity guidelines, current levels of physical activity in young people and the benefits of physical activity have proven beneficial in this regard. Developing students' knowledge and skills in how to plan and monitor their own physical activity programmes can be developed through effective modelling and the sharing of examples and templates. After students have begun to develop their understanding of the common barriers to participation and how these can be overcome, 'movement promoter' challenges can be used to encourage students to support others (i.e. peers, family) to be more active. Students have also reported the positive motivational influence of knowing what physical activities their teachers participate in, with particularly effective examples being visualised on notice boards or school plasma screens, along with other important physical activity messaging.

Assessment

With 'valuing a physically active life' being the main idea of HbPE, the affective domain should take priority when teaching and assessing students' progress. Key to affective learning is ensuring that approaches are self-referenced and focus on student development and progress, rather than comparison with others (Teraoka et al., 2021). A range of tools can be used to assess physical activity participation including physical activity diaries, student surveys, pedometers, activity tracking apps, heart-rate monitors, photographs and extra-curricular attendance registers. An understanding of students' attitudes to PE and physical activity can be gained through surveys, attitudinal scales and observing behaviours and effort during lessons. Cognitive development can be assessed through regular student questioning, observing their completion of practical tasks and activities and from in- and out-of-class learning tasks. Finally, social development can be readily observed in class and other physical activity settings as well as demonstrated through student diaries/reflections and/or photographs.

Box 5.6 The Pedagogy of HbPE

Considering the pedagogy of HbPE:
   How might you ensure the teaching, learning and assessment strategies employed in HbPE enable the four learning aspirations (habitual, motivated, informed and critical movers) to be achieved?

Conclusion

This chapter has explored the rationale and framework for the HbPE pedagogical model. The approach taken in HbPE purposefully contrasts with the emphasis typical in many health-related PE programmes and which appears to have had limited success in promoting healthy, active lifestyles among young people. Instead, HbPE's main idea seeks to improve health outcomes in young people through an emphasis on physical activity as a resource for life. There is now convincing evidence of the physical, social, emotional, personal and cognitive benefits of participation in physical activity which can genuinely enrich young people's lives. HbPE identifies four learning aspirations that support students to become habitual, motivated, informed and critical movers. To achieve these aspirations, the framework justified critical elements that support teaching and learning as well as key assumptions to guide teachers in the design and implementation of school-based programmes. A range of pedagogical considerations were shared, including teaching, learning and assessment strategies, followed by discussion concerning the selection of appropriate lesson content with respect to the types of physical activities that will enhance meaningfulness for students.

Summary and Recommendations

- Current approaches in PE are largely ineffective in promoting healthy, active lifestyles among young people. This, plus the growing use of pedagogical models in PE provide the rationale for a new pedagogical model for HbPE.
- HbPE has been developed 'with' teachers through a process of participatory action research as well as in line with theoretical and empirical research.
- HbPE's framework and strategies recontextualise how health-related PE might be taught in schools to more effectively emphasise the promotion of healthy, active lifestyles. We recommend that this recontextualisation (from fitness to physical activity) is the most effective action teachers could take in their health-related PE practice.
- Valuing a physically active life is aligned closely with the features of self-determination theory and meaningful PE, which require approaches that prioritise the affective learning domain.
- We recommend that health-related PE programmes support students to become habitual, motivated, informed and critical 'movers' through the alignment of goals, pedagogical approaches and subject content.
- We recommend that HbPE becomes a central and explicit area of the curriculum, revisited and developed throughout a student's PE journey, with each unit taught for a sustained period (12 weeks or longer). HbPE should incorporate lifetime and informal activities that are meaningful to students and available in the community.
- HbPE can be taught alongside other approaches and models in PE and across the school to support the promotion of health and physical activity among students.

Box 5.7 Next Steps

Based on the content of this chapter, and reflecting on your school's health-related PE practice:

1   Consider the extent to which HbPE has the potential to support health-related PE practice in your school and any barriers to its implementation.

> 2   If HbPE can support your practice, what steps might you
>   now take to implement this in your school? Identify a time-
>   line of actions (with colleagues) for developing a unit of
>   learning, lesson plans and associated resources which draw
>   on the main idea, learning aspirations, critical elements and
>   pedagogy of HbPE.

Note

1 Supervised by Ash Casey and Lorraine Cale.

Bibliography

Fletcher, T., Ní Chróinín, D., Gleddie, D., & Beni, S. (2021). *Meaningful Physical Education: An Approach for Teaching and Learning.* London: Routledge.

Haerens, L., Aelterman, N., Van den Berghe, L., De Meyer, J., Soenens, B., & Vansteenkiste, M. (2013). Observing physical education teachers' need-supportive interactions in classroom settings. *Journal of Sport and Exercise Psychology*, 35, 3–17.

References

Armour, K., & Harris, J. (2013). Making the case for developing new PE-for-health pedagogies. *Quest*, 65(2), 201–219.

Bailey, R., Hillman, C., Arent, S., & Petitpas, A. (2013). Physical activity: An underestimated investment in human capital? *Journal of Physical Activity and Health*, 10, 289–308.

Biddle, S., Mutrie, N., Gorely, T., & Faulkner, G. (2021). *Psychology of Physical Activity: Determinants, Wellbeing and Interventions.* 4th edn. London: Routledge.

Bowler, M. (2019). *Developing a Pedagogical Model for Health-Based Physical Education.* Doctoral Thesis. Loughborough University. Available at: https://dspace.lboro.ac.uk/2134/37704.

Bowler, M., & Sammon, P. (2020). Health-based physical education – A framework for promoting active lifestyles in children and young people. Part 1: Introducing a new pedagogical model for health-based physical education. *Physical Education Matters*, 15(3), 60–63.

Casey, A., & Kirk, D. (2021). *Models-Based Practice in Physical Education.* London: Routledge.

Fernandez-Rio, J. (2016). Health-based physical education: A model for educators. *Journal of Physical Education, Recreation and Dance*, 87(8), 5–7.

Fletcher, T., Ní Chróinín, D., Gleddie, D., & Beni, S. (2021). *Meaningful Physical Education: An Approach for Teaching and Learning*. London: Routledge.

Guthold, R., Stevens, G.A., Riley, L.M., & Bull, F.C. (2020). Global trends in insufficient physical activity among adolescents: A pooled analysis of 298 population-based surveys with 1.6 million participants. *Lancet Child & Adolescent Health*, 4(1), 23–35.

Haerens, L., Kirk, D., Cardon, G., & De Bourdeaudhuij, I. (2011). Toward the development of a pedagogical model for health-based physical education. *Quest*, 63, 321–338.

Harris, J., & Leggett, G. (2015). Testing, training and tensions: The expression of health within physical education curricula in secondary schools in England and Wales. *Sport, Education and Society*, 20(4), 423–441.

Hastie, P. (2010). Putting pedagogy back into sport pedagogy research: A case for more applied research in physical education'. Paper presented at the British Educational Research Association Physical Education and Sport Pedagogy Special Interest Group (BERA PESP SIG). Invisible College, University of Warwick, 31 August.

Kirk, D. (2010) *Physical Education Futures*. London: Routledge.

Kretchmar, R. (2006). Ten more reasons for quality physical education. *Journal of Physical Education, Recreation and Dance*, 77(9), 6–9.

Lally, P., Van Jaarsveld, C., Potts, H., & Wardle, J. (2010). How are habits formed: Modelling habit formation in the real world. *European Journal of Social Psychology*, 40(6), 998–1009.

Lund, J., & Tannehill, D. (Eds.). (2010). *Standards-Based Physical Education Curriculum Development*. 2nd edn. Sudbury, MA: Jones and Bartlett Publishers.

Martins, J., Marques, A., Sarmento, H., & Carreiro da Costa, F. (2015). Adolescents' perspectives on the barriers and facilitators of physical activity: A systematic review of qualitative studies. *Health Education Research*, 30(5), 742–755.

McConnell, K. (2015). Fitness and wellness education. In: J. Lund, & D. Tannehill (Eds.), *Standards-Based Physical Education Curriculum Development* (3rd edn., pp. 365–383). Burlington, MA: Jones & Bartlett Learning.

Metzler, M., McKenzie, T., Van der Mars, H., Barrett-Williams, S., & Ellis, R. (2013). Health Optimizing Physical Education (HOPE): A new curriculum for school programs – Part 1: Establishing the need and describing the model. *Journal of Physical Education, Recreation and Dance*, 84(4), 41–47.

Michie, S., Van Stralen, M., & West, R. (2011). The behaviour change wheel: A new method for characterising and designing behaviour change interventions. *Implementation Science*, 6, 42.

O'Connor, J., & Penney, D. (2021). Informal sport and curriculum futures: An investigation of the knowledge, skills and understandings for participation and the possibilities for physical education. *European Physical Education Review*, 27(1), 3–26.

Sammon, P. (2019). *Adopting a New Model for Health-Based Physical Education: The Impact of a Professional Development Programme on Teachers' Pedagogical Practice*. PhD Thesis. Loughborough University. Available at: https://doi.org/10.26174/thesis.lboro.8299685.

Sammon, P., & Bowler, M. (2020). Health-based physical education – A framework for promoting active lifestyles in children and young people. Part 2: Health-based physical education in practice. *Physical Education Matters*, 15(3), 64–66.

Siedentop, D. (1996). Valuing the physically active life: Contemporary and future directions. *Quest*, 48, 266–274.

Teixeira, P., Carraça, E., Markland, D., Silva, M., & Ryan, R. (2012). Exercise, physical activity, and self-determination theory: A systematic review. *International Journal of Behavioural Nutrition and Physical Activity*, 9(78), 1–30.

Teraoka, E., Jancer Ferreira, H., Kirk, D., & Bardid, F. (2021). Affective learning in physical education: A systematic review. *Journal of Teaching in Physical Education*, 40(3), 460–473.

Walton-Fisette, J., Sutherland, S., & Hill, J. (Eds.). (2019). *Teaching about Social Justice Issues in Physical Education*. Charlotte, NC: Information Age Publishing.

6 The Promoting Active Lifestyles (PAL) Project

An Approach in Focus

Jo Harris and Lorraine Cale

Introduction

This chapter focusses on a pedagogical approach to enhancing the promotion of physical activity in schools, entitled the Promoting Active Lifestyles (PAL) Project. The main aim of the Project was to create and implement approaches to promoting active lifestyles among young people which would help align PE trainees' and teachers' health-related philosophies and pedagogies (as discussed in Chapter 1). This alignment would assist in matching their aspirations for young people to lead physically active lives with effective practices to achieve this. Multiple factors influenced the development and features of this Project such as growing concerns about young people's health and about the expression of health within PE, plus awareness of inadequacies in health-related professional development and PE teachers' lack of appropriate pedagogies for effectively promoting active lifestyles (see Chapter 1 for a discussion of these).

This chapter initially outlines the key features and theoretical frameworks underpinning the PAL Project. This is followed by a description of PE trainees' and teachers' involvement in the Project which included the co-construction of principles and paradoxes associated with the promotion of active lifestyles. The PE trainees' and teachers' implementation of these and their influence on their health-related philosophies and pedagogies are then evidenced and discussed. The chapter concludes with a summary of the main findings arising from the Project and recommendations to support teachers in promoting active lifestyles in schools based on the principles, paradoxes and lessons learned.

After reading this chapter, you will be able to:

i   describe the key features of and theoretical frameworks underpinning the PAL Project;

DOI: 10.4324/9781003225904-6

ii outline PE trainees' and teachers' involvement in the Project and the main outcomes from their involvement;

iii identify and understand the relevance of the PAL principles and paradoxes to promoting active lifestyles among young people;

iv select and implement PAL principles and paradoxes within your school and PE curriculum and apply the recommendations arising from the Project.

Key Features of and Theoretical Frameworks Underpinning the PAL Project

Key features of the PAL Project were informed by reviews of school-based physical activity interventions (e.g. Golden & Earp, 2012; Kriemler et al., 2011; Salmon et al., 2007). The features included the Project's clear focus on a single health behaviour (physical activity) and a single setting (schools) and its pedagogical, multi-faceted whole-school approach to the promotion of active lifestyles among young people. An additional key feature was its flexible design, the purpose of which was to increase the accessibility of the Project across multiple school settings and populations and to enhance its sustainability. Reviews highlighted the public health potential of high quality, school-based physical activity interventions for increasing physical activity in youth (Kriemler et al., 2011), and revealed that interventions that are multi-faceted (e.g. increasing physical activity levels in PE as well as incorporating environmental changes) (Salmon et al., 2007), focus on certain topics or in particular settings, and which require little training and rely on less structured types of physical activity are more effective, successful and sustainable (Golden & Earp, 2012).

The theoretical framework underpinning the PAL Project was social cognitive theory which recognises the multiple influences on health behaviour (Bandura, 1986). Within this umbrella theory, a model which has been utilised in previous school-based physical activity interventions was adopted, the social ecological model (Hyndman et al., 2012; Langille & Rodgers, 2010). This model acknowledges the interactive characteristics of individuals and environments that underlie health outcomes (Sallis, Owen & Fisher, 2008) and emphasises that health behaviour is influenced by multiple levels associated with individual, social, environmental and policy factors (Salmon & King, 2010). The Project focussed in particular on the intrapersonal and interpersonal levels of the social ecological model (McLeroy et al., 1988) by providing professional development and ongoing support to PE trainees and teachers who are in a position to influence young people's health-related understandings, attitudes and behaviours.

PE Teachers' Involvement in the PAL Project

The PAL Project ran for four years and involved PE trainee and experienced teachers from a one year University-based secondary school Initial Teacher Education partnership in the East Midlands in England. At the beginning of each academic year in years 1–3, PE trainee teachers and school-based PE mentors (experienced PE teachers who support trainee teachers' development in schools) were invited to be involved in the Project. During years 2 and 3, the invitation was also sent to those involved in previous years. During the fourth year of the Project, no new invitations were made but those previously involved could continue their involvement. In total, 32 individuals joined the Project (26 as trainees and 6 as teachers) and 22 teachers remained with the Project throughout.

During the first year, the teachers participated in four, two-hour professional development sessions at the University every few months. These sessions addressed the known limited and limiting health discourses and approaches within PE. For example, the teachers were involved in discussions about the implications of global literature associated with the promotion of active lifestyles, such as that relating to whole-school approaches, physical activity for health recommendations, health-based PE and the role of fitness testing in promoting activity. The teachers were also introduced to some principles associated with promoting active lifestyles based on research-informed good practice (e.g. promoting active travel to school; teaching students how active they should be). They were then invited to co-construct additional activity-promoting principles and to implement any number of them in the schools in which they were employed or undertaking their school placements. These principles are presented later.

During the following three academic years, the teachers took part in a three hour University-based workshop during which the previously developed principles were again shared and they were encouraged to amend or add to them, and then implement any that were closely aligned with their school contexts and students' needs. From year 2 onwards, the teachers were also introduced to evidence-based contradictions associated with promoting active lifestyles (referred to as PAL paradoxes) and invited to think of additional such anomalies. Following this, the teachers were asked to review their own health-related philosophies and practices in light of these paradoxes, and were encouraged to use them to inform their own pedagogies as well as to try and influence the health-related philosophies and pedagogies of their colleagues/peers.

The professional development provided opportunities for the teachers to share and reflect on their experiences and they were encouraged to continue to do this via online groups to create a supportive community of practice (Wenger, 2000). The authors did not engage with these groups other than responding to requests from them (e.g. for additional resources). After three months, the teachers completed an online survey which focussed on their implementation of selected PAL principles and/or paradoxes, and any changes to their thinking or teaching about promoting active lifestyles. They also completed a survey at the end of each academic year which included previous questions and asked what had helped and hindered their implementation of the PAL principles/paradoxes. The teachers were further invited to be interviewed to discuss the impact of their involvement in the Project on themselves, their students and their schools. Interviews were conducted with 10 (out of a possible 22) teachers. Full details of the methodology adopted in the Project have been reported elsewhere (Harris, Cale & Hooper, 2020a, 2020b).

Box 6.1 The Design of the PAL Project

Reflect on the design of the PAL Project and consider the following questions:

1   Could this type of approach to pedagogical change work in your school?
2   What might help its adoption in your school? Is there anything that might hinder its adoption? If so, how can these obstacles be overcome?

PAL Principles and Paradoxes

In total, 20 general principles considered to support the promotion of active lifestyles among young people were co-constructed as part of the PAL Project. Of these, ten were categorised as whole-school and ten as PE-specific, as follows:

Whole-School PAL Principles

1 Include the physical activity for health guidelines for children in the teaching of Personal, Social, Health and Economic (PSHE) education (alongside other health guidelines) as well as in PE.
2 Discuss the promotion of active lifestyles, including marketing the 'one hour a day' physical activity guideline, with all staff, governors, students and parents/carers.
3 Put 'increasing physical activity levels' on the agenda of School Councils and encourage student representatives to propose ideas for achieving this.
4 Increase activity levels in non-PE lessons by having students move more within the learning environment (e.g. in the classroom or outdoors).
5 Promote active travel to school (cycling, walking, scooting) and ensure safe storage of cycles/scooters.
6 Ensure that physical activity facilities (including changing areas) are well managed, clean and safe.
7 Review the school's extra-curricular physical activity programme and consider how accessible/appealing it is for ALL students.
8 Encourage and reward teachers from all subjects to contribute to the school's extra-curricular programme.
9 Visibly raise the profile of physical activity in school (e.g. via noticeboards, newsletters, intranet/website, assemblies, media).
10 Develop good community links (e.g. with feeder/partner schools, local leisure centres and sports clubs) to increase the quality and quantity of physical activity opportunities for students.

PE-Specific PAL Principles

1 Limit/reduce time spent getting ready for/from PE lessons; maximise 'learning' time.
2 Meet the Association for Physical Education (afPE) guideline of students moving for 50%–80% of the available learning time (excluding changing and getting to/from venues) by limiting/reducing the time spent giving instructions and queueing/waiting to access equipment/resources.
3 Use the time spent getting to and from venues actively (e.g. walking briskly, jogging), as part of the warm up/cool down.
4 Teach students about the broad range of benefits (physical, psychological and social) of a healthy, active lifestyle, including the role of physical activity in healthy weight management.

5 Move students on to the next task without stopping the whole class, where appropriate.
6 Acknowledge, praise and reward effort and progress.
7 Include assessment of learning and progress in active ways (e.g. show me….; demonstrate….; shadow….).
8 Routinely inform students where they can be active within 3–5 miles of the school radius (in every unit of learning and via the school's intranet/library).
9 Teach students how active they should be, involve them in monitoring their activity levels so they become aware of how active they are, and inform them of multiple ways of increasing their activity levels.
10 Identify low active students and offer them (and their parents/carers) support/guidance/information and targeted/bespoke activity sessions.

PAL Paradoxes

The PE trainees and teachers were introduced to the following evidence-based PAL paradoxes:

• The promotion of active lifestyles is usually prominent in teachers' philosophies of PE, yet it is much less evident in PE curricula. For example, while PE teachers often claim to encourage and educate about long-term engagement in physical activity, their written and taught schemes/units do not necessarily reflect this.
• PE lessons offer regular opportunities to be active, yet activity levels in PE are generally low. For example, while students may have regular PE lessons, it seems that they are not particularly active during PE lessons.
• PE teachers often claim to use fitness testing to promote activity, yet many students dislike and learn little from fitness testing. For example, fitness testing is frequently incorporated into PE curricula to encourage students to be active, but many do not enjoy the experience and gain limited knowledge and understanding from it.
• There is an expectation that teachers increase students' understanding of health, activity and fitness but many children have misunderstandings about these which could hinder the promotion of active lifestyles. For example, students have opportunities to enhance their understanding about physical activity from PE lessons, but many have misconceptions associated with this such as needing to run fast to be healthy.

The following additional paradox associated with the promotion of active lifestyles and one which focusses on the use and influence of digital technologies to support PE pedagogies for health (as discussed in Chapter 7) was proposed and developed by the PE trainees and teachers during the Project:

• Technology can help motivate students to be active, but it can also reduce activity levels. For example, the use of activity trackers in PE lessons can encourage some students to be more active yet the use of tablets for demonstration and analysis of actions can result in less activity.

Each paradox was presented in the form of a resource which included a statement about the contradictory issue, a summary of the literature associated with contrasting perspectives on the issue, and reflective questions about what might be done to address the paradox.

Box 6.2 The PAL Principles and Paradoxes

Reflect on the PAL principles and paradoxes and consider the following questions:

1   Which, if any, of the whole-school PAL principles could be implemented in your school? How might these improve the promotion of active lifestyles in your school?
2   Which, if any, of the PE-specific PAL principles could be implemented in your department? How might these improve your teaching/promotion of active lifestyles?
3   Are any of the PAL paradoxes of particular interest to you and if so, why?
4   Which, if any, of the PAL paradoxes might interest your colleagues? Is a collaborative approach to addressing some of these a possibility in your school?

Outcomes of the PAL Project

A summary of the key outcomes of the PAL Project is reported here; further details have been published elsewhere (Harris, Cale & Hooper, 2020a, 2020b).

Positive Perspectives

All the teachers involved in the PAL Project were positive about its overall approach to promoting active lifestyles among young people. Typical views included 'It's straightforward, not like previous programmes that were a burden' and 'We liked the freedom and flexibility of this approach'. The co-construction of both 'whole-school' and 'PE-specific' principles suggests that the trainees and teachers appreciated the multiple and interactive influences that underlie health outcomes. Collectively, the principles reflected the Project's underpinning theoretical framework and model, acknowledging the influence of a range of experiences, actions and factors on children's physical activity behaviour (Salmon & King, 2010) such as access to wide-ranging and appealing extra-curricular and community-based programmes and the importance of involving teachers of other subjects and parents/carers.

Practical Principles

All teachers considered the PAL principles to be 'practical', 'manageable' and 'easy to put into practice' and were able to implement a selection of them, albeit predominantly PE-specific ones. For example, teachers reported to have reduced changing time and thereby increased learning time, to have used active assessment during lessons, and to have increased activity levels in lessons by reducing episodes of whole class instruction. Some of the experienced teachers had also adopted a collaborative, 'departmental' approach to implementing the PE principles. The PAL principles which worked especially well in this respect included reducing changing time and 'teacher talk', utilising active plenaries and encouraging students to jog to the lesson venue as part of the warm up.

The greater implementation of PE-specific over whole-school principles confirms Craig and colleagues' (2016) finding that teachers generally pay more attention to subject-specific and pragmatic issues than to generic curriculum ambitions such as the promotion of health. Nevertheless, a small number of experienced teachers were able to implement some whole-school principles such as raising the profile of physical activity using posters around the school and incorporating physical activity as a topic within the PSHE programme.

In contrast, some trainee teachers commented on challenges to implementing whole-school principles relating to their career stage, making remarks such as 'I'm only a trainee' and 'It's difficult for me as a trainee to go beyond the changes I can implement within my own lessons'.

These challenges reflect the literature on occupational socialisation which reveals that trainee and early career teachers can be hindered by situational workplace constraints (Curtner-Smith, 2001). Furthermore, their plans can be subdued by neoliberalist school cultures characterised by accountability, work intensification, performance appraisal, regulation of teacher competence and competition (Loh & Hu, 2014).

A further outcome of the PAL Project related to additional and unexpected benefits beyond increasing students' physical activity. Examples teachers cited included improved student behaviour and enjoyment and students' positive responses to some of the new practices such as active assessment. These unexpected benefits inevitably reflect the complex and interconnected nature of teaching and learning. They also evidence positive student responses to pedagogical change, although it should be noted that these were based on the teachers' perceptions only.

A particularly positive outcome of the PAL Project was that all the PE trainees and teachers reported major changes to their thinking and teaching about active lifestyles which they believe led to them becoming more effective promoters of physical activity. Examples of these changes included: referencing health and well-being more in lessons; realising that the promotion of active lifestyles is the responsibility of all teachers and recognising that health needs to be a key pillar and an on-going theme of PE and the wider school curriculum. Furthermore, many intended to implement selected PAL principles in the future. Comments relating to this included: 'I'm going to continue with the PE principles I've had success with so far and…try out some whole school ones' and 'We're going to continue with the principles…already introduced and…teach about the physical activity guidelines in PSHE'.

Perplexing PAL Paradoxes

All the trainees and teachers found the PAL paradoxes interesting and thought-provoking. Typical terms used to describe the paradoxes included: 'fascinating', 'perplexing', 'surprising' and 'baffling' with the teachers clearly keen to address them. One teacher explained that he did not 'want to turn into a hypocrite, saying one thing and doing another', one stated 'We can't live with these contradictions', and another claimed the paradoxes were 'going to change a lot of' what they do. Most of the teachers urgently wanted to 'solve' the contradictions posed by the paradoxes. Typical comments included: 'I decided that my department needed to do something about this straight away' and 'This all needs sorting out and quickly. It's our responsibility to match what we say and do'. Indeed, these comments suggest that the teachers felt some degree of accountability for the contradictions and considered themselves capable of changing their own health-related thinking and practices and potentially also those of their colleagues. This highlights the key role of teacher agency (i.e. the potential to act in the interplay between personal capacities and contexts) in bringing about change and the importance of reflection in the process (Leijen, Pedeste & Lepp, 2020).

Some trainees and teachers reported a degree of success in influencing colleagues' and/or peers' health-related thinking and practices such as adding 'in more links to pupils' lifestyles'. A number of teachers stated that the paradoxes 'made us all re-think what we're doing' and 'prompted a lot of good debate and action'. However, some of the trainee and early career teachers in particular experienced frustration and difficulties with attempting to change the health-related thinking and practices of their peers and/or colleagues, with reports of colleagues being 'stuck in their ways' and not responsive to change or willing to put in the time, effort and energy required. Issues such as resistance to change, challenging workloads and limited time have previously been reported to restrict the attention afforded to health outcomes in PE (Cale, 2021). Such constraints reflect the tension between pursuing education and health outcomes in schools (as discussed in Chapter 1) and suggest that this area of work continues to be complex and challenging, even for experienced teachers.

Despite the complexity and on-going challenges, the collective and positive outcomes of the PAL Project indicate that it helped to align the trainees' and teachers' health-related philosophies and pedagogies which resulted in positive changes to their students' experiences of physical activity within PE and the wider school setting. This suggests that an explicit focus on the intrapersonal and interpersonal levels of the social ecological model (Langille & Rodgers, 2010) through support for PE trainees and teachers (and, in turn, their colleagues and peers) can lead to improvements in their effectiveness as promoters of physical activity. This is consistent with the findings of Weaver and colleagues (2016, 2018) in the United States and Bowler (2019) and Sammon (2019) in the United Kingdom (see Chapters 4 and 5 for details of Bowler and Sammon's work), where similar improvements were detected following the implementation of new practices and a new pedagogical model respectively.

Project Strengths

The sustained engagement of many of the PE teachers throughout the duration of the PAL Project was undoubtedly reflective of its inclusive, flexible and low-burden approach. Sustainability was further enhanced by its support system, as has been found in the implementation of previous school-based physical activity interventions (Naylor et al., 2015). The Project sought to empower teachers by involving them in co-constructing knowledge and curriculum development, avoiding a top down approach and the rigidity that has previously been identified with ineffective school programmes (Forman et al., 2009). In these ways, the PAL Project avoided the limitations of much professional development in PE (Keay, Carse & Jess, 2019) and built on key characteristics of effective professional development such as acknowledging the complexity of the learning process, prioritising context and contemporary challenges and bridging research/theory-practice in innovative ways (Armour et al., 2017). It also addressed the known 'conundrum' of PE teachers' lack of engagement with health-related professional development associated with limited awareness of gaps in their health-related knowledge and understanding (Alfrey, Cale & Webb, 2012).

Box 6.3 Improving the PAL Project

Reflecting on the PAL Project, consider the following questions:

1 Can you identify any particular strengths and limitations of the Project?
2 How might the Project be further developed and improved in the future?
3 What further support is needed by PE teachers to effectively promote active lifestyles among young people?

Conclusion

The PAL Project's research-informed approach disturbed current health-related thinking and practices and led to evidence-based teaching in this area. Transformative and enduring changes to the PE trainees' and teachers' health-related philosophies and pedagogies were achieved by creating the conditions for better aligning teachers' philosophy with their practices. This involved facilitating PE teachers' professional autonomy and encouraging critical, creative and personalised responses to change agendas associated with health and PE. The Project thereby represented an authentic and constructive response to calls for critical, sophisticated approaches to addressing public health goals within an educational setting (Kirk, 2006) and for evidence-based PE-for-health pedagogies (Armour & Harris, 2013; Puhse et al., 2011). It also addressed neoliberalist concerns associated with the privileging of reductive health-related practices in PE centred on measurable outcomes, accountability and heightened surveillance (Evans, 2014; Macdonald, 2011). Importantly, it showed that, even with tensions between the pursuit of education and health outcomes in schools and the constraints of a neoliberalist context, significant teacher change is possible. This is promising given that previous research on PE teachers' professional development in this area has cited teacher engagement and teacher change to be particularly challenging (Alfrey, Cale & Webb, 2012).

Summary and Recommendations

- A key aim of the PAL Project was to help PE trainees and teachers align their aspirations for young people to lead physically active lives with their practices, within the context of a whole-school approach.
- The Project involved the co-construction and implementation of PAL principles and paradoxes, considered to be associated with the promotion of active lifestyles among young people.
- All the PE trainees and teachers involved in the Project viewed the PAL principles positively and were able to implement some of them. They also found the PAL paradoxes interesting and perplexing and expressed a keen desire to address them.
- Many of the PE trainees and teachers described how their involvement in the Project led to transformative and enduring changes to their health-related philosophies and pedagogies and some reported being able to influence colleagues/peers' health-related philosophies and pedagogies.
- The Project resulted in closer alignment between PE trainees' and teachers' health-related philosophies and pedagogies which they believed led to them becoming more effective promoters of physical activity.
- A recommendation arising from the Project is for PE teachers to discuss their department's health-related philosophy and ensure that it aligns with pedagogies which effectively support the promotion of active lifestyles.
- Teachers are also encouraged to raise awareness among colleagues of the PAL principles and paradoxes and select and implement those which they feel could effectively be applied to their context.

- Teachers are advised to routinely and regularly reflect with colleagues and students on the impact of the wider school and PE curriculum on young people's attitudes towards and involvement in physical activity, and be open-minded and prepared to make on-going activity-promoting changes to the design, organisation and delivery of the curriculum.

Bibliography

Harris, J., & Cale, L. (2019). *Promoting Active Lifestyles in Schools.* Leeds: Human Kinetics.

Harris, J., Cale, L., Casey, A., Tyne, A., & Samarai, B. (2016). Promoting active lifestyles in schools: the PAL project. *Physical Education Matters*, 11(3), 52–53.

Harris, J., Cale, L., & Hooper, O. (2020a). The Promoting Active Lifestyles (PAL) Project: A principle-based approach to pedagogical change. *The Curriculum Journal*, special issue. https://doi.org/10.1002/curj.99

Harris, J., Cale, L., & Hooper, O. (2020b). Prompting pedagogical change through promoting active lifestyles (PAL) paradoxes. *International Journal of Environmental Research and Public Health*, 17, 7965. https://doi.org/10.3390/ijerph 17217965

References

Alfrey, L., Cale, L., & Webb, L. (2012). Physical education teachers' continuing professional development in health-related exercise. *Physical Education and Sport Pedagogy*, 17(5), 477–491.

Armour, K., & Harris, J. (2013). Making the case for developing new PE-for-health pedagogies. *Quest*, 65(2), 201–219.

Armour, K., Quennerstedt, M., Chambers, F., & Makopoulou, K. (2017). What is 'effective' CPD for contemporary physical education teachers? A Deweyan framework. *Sport, Education and Society*, 22(7), 799–811.

Bandura, A. (1986). *Social Foundations of Thought and Action: A Social Cognitive Theory.* Englewood Cliffs, NJ: Prentice-Hall.

Bowler, M.T (2019). *Developing a Pedagogical Model for Health-based Physical Education.* Doctoral Thesis. Loughborough University. https://hdl.handle.net/2134/37704.

Cale, L. (2021). Physical education's journey on the road to health. *Sport, Education and Society*, 26(5), 486–499.

Craig, M., Thorburn, M., Mulholland, R., Jess, M., & Horrell, A. (2016). Understanding professional issues in physical education – A Scottish insight. *Scottish Educational Review*, 48(2), 80–100.

Curtner-Smith, M.D. (2001). The occupational socialisation of a first-year physical education teacher with a teaching orientation. *Sport, Education and Society*, 6, 81–105.

Evans, J. (2014). Neoliberalism and the future for a socio-educative physical education. *Physical Education and Sport Pedagogy*, 19(5), 545–558.

Forman, S.G., Olin, S.S., Hoagwood, K.E., et al. (2009). Evidence-based interventions in schools: Developers' views of implementation barriers and facilitators. *School Mental Health*, 1, 26–36.

Golden, S.D., & Earp, J.A.L. (2012). Social ecological approaches to individuals and their contexts: Twenty years of health promotion interventions. *Health Education & Behavior*, 39(3), 364–372.

Hyndman, B., Telford, A., Finch, C.F., & Benson, A.C. (2012). Moving physical activity beyond the school classroom: A social-ecological insight for teachers of the facilitators and barriers to students' non-curricular physical activity. *Australian Journal of Teacher Education*, 37(2), 1.

Keay, J., Carse, N., & Jess, M. (2019). Understanding teachers as complex professional learners. *Professional Development in Education*, 45(1), 125–137.

Kirk, D. (2006). The obesity 'crisis' and school physical education. *Sport, Education and Society*, 11(2), 121–133.

Kriemler, S., Meyer, U., van Sluijs, E.M.F., Andersen, L.B., & Martin, B.W. (2011). Effect of school-based interventions on physical activity and fitness in children and adolescents: a review of reviews and systematic update. *British Journal of Sports Medicine*, 45, 923–930.

Langille, J.L.D., & Rodgers, W.M. (2010). Exploring the influence of a social-ecological model on school-based physical activity. *Health Education and Behaviour*, 37(6), 879–894.

Leijen, A., Pedaste, M., & Lepp, L. (2020). Teacher agency following the ecological model: How it is achieved and how it could be strengthened by different types of reflection. *British Journal of Educational Studies*, 68, 295–310.

Loh, J., & Hu, G. (2014). Subdued by the system: Neoliberalism and the beginning teacher. *Teaching and Teacher Education*, 41, 13–21.

Macdonald, D. (2011). Like a fish in water: Physical education policy and practice in the era of neoliberal globalization. *Quest*, 63(1), 36–45.

McLeroy, K.R., Bibeau, D., Steckler, A., & Glanz, K. (1988). An ecological perspective on health promotion programs. *Health Education Quarterly*, 15, 351–377.

Naylor, P.J., Nettlefold, L., Race, D., Hoy, C., Ashe, M.C., Higgins, J.W., & McKay, H.A. (2015). Implementation of school based physical activity interventions: A systematic review. *Preventive Medicine*, 72, 95–115.

Puhse, U., Barker, D., Brettschneider, W.D. et al. (2011). International approaches to health-oriented physical education: Local health debates and differing conceptions of health. *International Journal of Physical Education*, 3, 2–15.

Sallis, J. F., Owen, N., & Fisher, E.B. (2008). Ecological models of health behaviour. In: K. Glanz, B.K. Rimer, & K. Viswanath (Eds.), *Health Behaviour and Health Education: Theory, Research and Practice* (pp. 465–486). San Francisco, CA: Jossey-Bass.

Salmon, J., Booth, M.L., Phongsavan, P., Murphy, N., & Timperio, A. (2007). Promoting physical activity participation among children and adolescents. *Epidemiological Reviews*, 29, 144–159.

Salmon, J., & King, A.C. (2010). Population approaches to increasing physical activity and reducing sedentary behaviour among children and adults. In: D. Crawford, R.W. Jeffrey, K. Ball, & J. Brug (Eds.), *Obesity Epidemiology: From Aetiology to Public Health* (pp. 186–207). Oxford University Press. DOI: 10.1093/acprof:oso/9780199571512.003.0012

Sammon, P. (2019). *Adopting a New Model for Health-based Physical Education: The Impact of a Professional Development Programme on Teachers' Pedagogical Practice*. Doctoral Thesis. Loughborough University. https://doi.org/10.26174/thesis.lboro.8299686

Weaver, R.G., Webster, C.A., Beets, M.W., Brazendale, K., Chandler, J., Schisler, L., & Aziz, M. (2018). Initial outcomes of a participatory-based, competency-building approach to increasing physical education teachers' physical activity promotion and students' physical activity: A pilot study. *Health Education & Behavior*, 45(3), 359–370.

Weaver, R.G., Webster, C.A., Erwin, H., Beighle, A., Beets, M.W., Choukroun, H., & Kaysing, N. (2016). Modifying the system for observing fitness instruction time to measure teacher competencies related to physical activity promotion: SOFIT+. *Journal of Physical Activity and Health*, 20, 121–130.

Wenger, E. (2000). *Communities of Practice: Learning, Meaning and Identity*. Cambridge: Cambridge University Press.

7   The Role of Physical Education and the Physical Education Teacher in a Digital Age

Victoria Goodyear and Kathleen Armour

Introduction

This chapter aims to generate new ways of thinking about PE and the PE teacher in a digital age. The proliferation of digital technologies and social media platforms and the generation of vast amounts of easily accessible health-related content and physical activity instruction, present a real challenge to the ways in which we conceptualise PE in young people's lives. We have long known that 'traditional' PE fails to meet the needs of many learners, so could PE in a digital era be reimagined in ways that address some of these challenges?

After reading this chapter you will be able to:

i   understand how young people today learn;
ii explain how the design, organisation and delivery of PE could be adapted to take advantage of digital affordances;
iii recognise how initial teacher training and continuing professional development (CPD) in PE could be changed in order to better prepare teachers to operate effectively in a digital age.

Young People and Learning about Physical Activity and Health

Young people's lives are now saturated by digital technologies (Shapiro, 2019). On a daily basis young people spend hours gaming, streaming, using their smartphones and/or interacting through social media. In many of their homes, smart devices help to regulate daily activities such as lighting, temperature, visitors, shopping, physical activity, sleep and much more. The use of digital technologies can therefore no longer be understood as a binary in which young people's lives are divided into digital and non-digital, or screen and non-screen time.

DOI: 10.4324/9781003225904-7

Digital technologies are integrated seamlessly into living for young people and, as such, are key contexts through which relationships, identities and cognitive processes are developed (Harrison, 2021). Accordingly, young people are more likely to have digitised habits, actions and behaviours compared to previous generations, and will probably differ in the ways in which they process information, express themselves, interact and manage and organise their daily activities. The important point here is that in this digital era, the characteristics of today's youth present a real challenge to the traditional role of PE in their lives.

Traditionally PE has been seen as a key context for young people to learn about physical activity and health (Harris et al., 2016). PE teachers have often been regarded as health-related role models who can inspire and help young people to engage with physical activity (Landi, 2017; Powell & Fitzpatrick, 2013). Yet, for some young people the context has changed. The accessibility of health-related social media content and health and fitness apps means that learning about health is no longer primarily a scheduled learning activity in school that is initiated and led by teachers but can be more self-directed. Young people can select and engage with content that is relevant to their needs and interests at specific moments in time (Chambers & Sandford, 2018; Rich et al., 2020).

International evidence shows that young people use social media to access content related to physical activity, diet, body image and mental health (Goodyear & Armour, 2019). Research has also shown that many young people experiment with workouts and recipes using content accessed from apps such as MyFitnessPal, FitBit, Pinterest and Apple Health (Rich et al., 2020). Further, there is a trend for young people to watch gamers play e-sports such as Fortnite or League of Legends on Twitch, Discord, YouTube or Facebook Live (Shapiro, 2019). In these co-viewing situations, young people can develop a form of rhetoric knowledge, where gamers act as 'role models' who can be studied and emulated in similar ways to – perhaps – elite sports people such as a famous footballer (Harrison, 2021). Hence, young people can learn about health and physical activity through accessible digital technologies, and from individuals other than PE teachers.

Taking this analysis further, the interactive functionalities of contemporary digital/online environments actively promote co-learning. Digital technologies such as smartphones, tablets, apps, digital/online games and social media provide opportunities to interact, collaborate, share information and resources, engage with critical thinking and access peer support (Krutka & Carpenter, 2016). Hence, digital technologies facilitate an array of learning experiences including collaborative knowledge construction, the hybridisation of expertise, relational development, peer support and social and civic learning (Greenhow & Lewin, 2015; Krutka & Carpenter, 2016). Furthermore, digital technologies enable young people to develop new knowledge, skills and behaviours through authentic engagement in play, repetition, scenarios, immersive experiences and social evaluation, within public, private and global spaces, and with known or unknown online 'friends' (Shapiro, 2019). Digital technologies, therefore, present vast opportunities for young people to learn in spaces that are relevant, meaningful and personalised for them and, critically, that do not always require a public display of ability or competence.

Ultimately, young people's attitudes towards physical activity and health, and what and how young people do, learn and understand in relation to health, are being continuously shaped and re-shaped by how they engage with digital technologies. In this context, there is a need to consider how best PE might be re-structured and re-organised and how PE teachers might be trained differently to meet the new needs of young people in a digital age.

Box 7.1 The Use of Digital Technologies in Your Practice

Reflect on how you use digital technologies in your practice and consider the following questions:

1 What are the main digital technologies you use within your PE lessons, and why?
2 How do you use digital technologies to promote health-related learning within your lessons?
3 To what extent are your uses of digital technologies in PE tailored to young people's interests and effective in supporting health-related learning?

Learning Attributes of PE in a Digital Age

It is widely agreed that a core aim of PE is to promote and prepare young people for lifelong engagement in physical activity (Ennis, 2017). In many schools, the key starting point for the design of PE is the curriculum and its delivery (Kirk, 2020). While there are localised innovations (Quennerstedt, 2013), it has been argued that in most schools the PE curriculum tends to be outdated, and based on curricula developed in the 1950s and 1960s and the cultures, customs and priorities of that era (Kirk, 2020). Indeed, in many schools PE curricula are grounded in the post-Second World War military traditions of sport, skills/techniques, fitness and command-based approaches (Kirk, 2020; Quennerstedt, 2013) (see Table 7.1). These practices have endured in PE even though evidence shows that they exclude many learners because of the prioritisation of white, male, heterosexual, fit and technocratic views of health and the body (Harris et al., 2016; Landi, 2017; Powell & Fitzpatrick, 2013). Reports from adults on their experiences of PE also provide evidence that, for many people, PE taught as sport, skills/techniques and fitness was a deterrent to physical activity engagement in adult life (Ladwig, Vazou & Malcolm, 2018). These findings are further supported by global statistics on the prevalence of physical inactivity in adolescent and adult populations (see, e.g. World Health Organisation, 2020). All of this suggests that current/traditional PE provision is continuing to fail to achieve one of its core aims for many young people.

Despite a growing body of work concerned with digital health technologies in young people's lives and related informal learning opportunities (see Goodyear & Armour, 2019; Greenhow et al., 2019), little serious attention has been given to the form and nature of digital health-related learning in PE. Across the globe PE programmes have tended to focus on embedding the use of different devices, apps and networks within the 'traditional' curriculum (Casey, Goodyear & Armour, 2016; Koekoek and Hilvoorde, 2018). To date, the literature has mainly reported on how PE teachers use digital technologies to meet pre-defined curriculum outcomes related to sport, skills or fitness, and/or how PE teachers have used digital devices to improve student engagement (Casey, Goodyear & Armour, 2016; Koekoek & Hilvoorde, 2018). These studies tend to oversimplify what we know about how young people use digital technologies for informal learning (Greenhow et al., 2019), and fail to consider how PE can enrich and support young people's formal and informal health-related learning through digital technologies (Chambers & Sandford, 2018; Goodyear & Armour, 2019). The influx of digital technologies into our daily lives should spur the PE profession to think differently about the relevance and appropriateness of PE provision for young people today. There is a need to think beyond simply adding the latest 'gizmos and gadgets' to our current understanding of PE and, instead, rethink how we view young people and appreciate the holistic and integrated nature of digital technologies in their lives today.

It has long been argued that the starting point for the design of PE should be young people and their complex, diverse and individual learning needs, rather than the curriculum and/or specific delivery methods or models (Armour, 2014; Casey, Goodyear & Armour, 2016). In this way, PE content, teaching methods and learning experiences can be adapted or radically reimagined to be effective for contemporary cultures, customs and priorities (Armour, 2014; Casey, Goodyear & Armour, 2016). One way to structure our thinking about a different approach to PE in a digital age is to focus on learning attributes.

A learning attribute can be defined as a key characteristic of learning, such as feedback, assessment or knowledge acquisition (Greenhow & Lewin, 2015). The concept of learning attributes is grounded in the theories of social constructivism and connectivism (Greenhow & Lewin, 2015), and builds on the work of Colley, Hodkinson and Malcolm (2003) on formal and informal learning contexts. A focus on learning attributes reminds us that learning is situated in the prevailing context of circumstances, activities and culture (constructivism), and that learning is a process of creating connections, networks and relationships (connectivism) (Greenhow & Lewin, 2015). Underpinning these concepts is the assumption that learning with digital technologies cannot be abstracted from other aspects of young people's lives. Thus, learning happens simultaneously across the contexts of digital technologies, home, school and community (Greenhow et al., 2019) and in both formal and informal contexts (Greenhow & Lewin, 2015). To be effective in supporting young people's learning with digital technologies, a focus on learning attributes suggests that PE needs to take into account young people's wider learning ecologies and context dependent forms of health-related learning.

To move the debate forward, we have proposed some learning attributes that could be appropriate for PE in a digital age (see Table 7.1) and compared them with those applicable to traditional PE and health-related education settings. The proposed learning attributes bridge aspects of: (i) young people's informal learning via digital health-related technologies (as outlined in the Section on 'Young People and Learning about Physical Activity and Health'); and (ii) the learning attributes of PE reflected in current PE curricula (as discussed at the start of the Section on 'Learning Attributes of PE in a Digital Age'). This approach has been grounded in the framing of ecologies of learning as suggested by Greenhow and Lewin (2016) and Colley, Hodkinson and Malcolm (2003). From this perspective,

Table 7.1 Learning Attributes of PE in a Digital Age

	Learning Attributes of PE (<2022)	*Learning Attributes of Health-Related Digital Technologies*	*Learning Attributes for PE in a Digital Age*
Purpose (intentional/ unintentional)	To prepare young people for lifelong engagement in physical activity Pre-defined learning outcomes (curriculum, standards, public health)	To engage with peers, play and/or enquire into the body Self-/socially determined outcomes	To support and enrich young people's health-related learning through digital technologies Co-produced outcomes between teacher and student
Process (structure, pedagogy, support, assessment)	Teacher-initiated and led Teacher as expert/authority Teacher-driven assessment Exclusive Team/group-based Homogenised Competitive Repetitive	Self-/peer initiated and led Expertise via participation Social evaluation Inclusive Collaborative Personalised Experimentation Play Repetitive Scenarios Rhetoric knowledge[a]	Collaborative teaching practices Peer-based pedagogies Peer role models Agency Empowering Personalised Rhetoric knowledge Self-regulation Self-social evaluation
Location/Context (norms and structure – e.g. timetables)	School-based School-centric engagement Time restricted (e.g. 2 lessons per week) Public space	Online, ubiquitous, ritual Family engagement Accessibility and immediacy (24/7 – open ended) Public and private spaces Immersive Global	Asynchronous and synchronous Public and private Mass engagement (national, global) Physical and virtual contexts Connect home, school and community

(Continued)

	Learning Attributes of PE (<2022)	*Learning Attributes of Health-Related Digital Technologies*	*Learning Attributes for PE in a Digital Age*
Content (high stakes knowledge – leisure interests)	Sport Games Skills/techniques Health/fitness	Body image Identity Relationships Mental wellbeing Health/fitness	Dynamic and have integrity to young people's health-related needs and interests, e.g. Sport Games Health/fitness Identity Relationships Mental wellbeing

[a] The ability to analyse and act on understandings of audiences, purposes and contexts in creating and comprehending text or visual information.

it is unhelpful to separate out different contexts of learning, and more sensible to consider the opportunities for learning that span across contexts and time points. As a result, our proposed learning attributes for PE in a digital age are grounded in an analysis of the different contexts of learning for physical activity and health as experienced by young people, as well as the opportunities for learning across both informal and formal contexts. Four main categories were used to identify the different attributes of learning: (i) purpose (intentional/unintentional); (ii) process (structure, pedagogy, support and assessment); (iii) location (including norms and structures, such as timetables); and (iv) content (high stakes knowledge – to leisure interests) (Table 7.1).

What follows are two illustrative case study examples of young people's engagement with health-related digital technologies that, we argue, present a major challenge to the current nature and form of PE provision. The case studies presented are analysed in the context of learning attributes in order to challenge the PE profession to think differently about PE in a digital age.

Case Study 1: Joe Wicks '#PEwithJOE'

#PEwithJOE began in March 2020 in response to the COVID-19 pandemic and the first United Kingdom (UK) lockdown.[1] As was the case in many countries, during this time schools were closed, there were limited resources and support for home-schooling, and most households were restricted to leaving their home once a day for exercise. #PEwithJOE involved free workouts hosted by Joe Wicks (a qualified personal trainer) on his YouTube channel 'The Body Coach' every Monday–Friday at 9am. The workouts focussed on different fitness exercises that involved no equipment such as squats, burpees, lunges, dancing or high knees, and were intended to be completed by all abilities and ages in the home. The sessions also incorporated learning from other subjects such as English, Maths or Geography and included concepts, quizzes or problems related to these areas. Overall, #PEwithJOE lasted one year and involved 115 workouts that had over 100 million views. At its peak, more than 955,000 people were exercising together at the same time and #PEwithJOE broke the world record for the largest ever number of participants engaging with a live streamed workout.[2]

Unlike traditional forms of PE, the *purpose* of engaging with #PEwithJOE was largely self-determined (or determined by parents/carers) and there were no pre-defined learning outcomes. The *process* of learning was teacher-led and aimed to be inclusive, using 'basic' movements that were repeated over a specified time period (e.g. 30 seconds). Joe Wicks also attempted to personalise learner engagement by providing 'shout outs' of encouragement to specific individuals, commenting on the live YouTube feed discussion board, and by adapting the different movements for different abilities. The *context* of learning was online, where engagement took place in a global public community at a specified time each day and in the privacy of the home. Participants were not visible to others but could participate with other family members such as parents/carers and siblings. In terms of *content*, the sessions centred mainly around basic exercises and aspects of High Intensity Interval Training and there was an explicit focus on fitness and achieving broader goals linked to physical and mental wellbeing.

This approach to engaging young people has a number of serious limitations. For example, there is no direct focus on learning which is clearly an expectation of curricular subjects. Moreover, it is impossible for the 'teacher' to support learners if exercises are performed incorrectly, and the content is necessarily limited which has the potential to exclude some learners.[3] On the other hand, and accepting its limitations, the PE profession might usefully learn some lessons from the success of this highly popular initiative. In essence, 'PE' became 'cool' and part of a very positive national conversation in a way that traditional PE arguably never has. Whereas the restrictions of the pandemic provided a specific context in which #PEwithJOE could flourish, and Joe Wicks himself already had an element of online celebrity status, we argue that its success should not be dismissed too quickly. At the very least we should recognise that #PEwithJOE was successful in promoting physical activity engagement and enjoyment and that it was a digital-first and mass approach to PE that caught national and international imagination.

Given the above, it can be claimed that #PEwithJOE highlights new opportunities for teachers to support physical activity

engagement through a particular approach to digital personalisation, and both asynchronous and synchronous digital experiences. In particular, the #PEwithJOE sessions connected
home, family and school and used online mediums to support
participation in physical activity with family members in public
(digital) and private spaces. Without accepting this approach as
an educational panacea, and with acute recognition of its limitations and potential pitfalls, it seems that teachers could build
on and enhance the approach to such online workouts to enrich
young people's health-related learning. For example, we should
consider ways in which we can use these digital mediums as a
pedagogical resource to show how to perform (or not) specific
movements, help young people to critically evaluate online ma-
terial and/or to make cross-curricula links with other subjects.
These strategies could be of particular value where teachers experience key challenges related to a lack of specialist training,
qualifications and confidence for teaching PE, restricted equip-
ment and space for PE, and the prioritisation of core and Science, Technology, Engineering and Maths (STEM) subjects in
schools.

Case Study 2: The British E-Sports Championships

The British E-sports Championships is a competitive video
gaming competition for students aged 12+ in schools and col-
leges across the UK.[4] Tournaments include Rocket League[5]
(Vehicular soccer video game), Overwatch[6] (Multi-player first-
person shooter game) and League of Legends[7] (Multi-player
battle arena game). School teams play against other schools
virtually after school, but each team plays together in the same
classroom on consoles or computers. The best in-game moments
as a team or individual are shared across the British E-sports
YouTube and social media gaming channels (e.g. Twitch) and the
final is streamed live. In 2020, more than 250 school teams from
across the UK took part in the British E-sports Championships
and in some schools whole-school competitions have been initiated.[8] Young people have reported that e-sports benefits their

mental health and provides a space for stress relief, to have fun, share ideas and develop their social skills and confidence.[9] In addition, teachers have reported that participation in e-sports has improved young people's learning in literacy and maths, and students' strategical and tactical thinking, teamwork skills and the ability to cope with defeat in PE.[10] Moreover, these benefits have been reported in both mainstream and alternative provision schools with vulnerable youth.[11]

The purpose of engaging with e-sports is largely self-determined and focussed on enjoyment and play, as participation tends to occur as an after-school voluntary activity. The process of learning is predominantly determined by the game that sets the rules and penalties within the game. In turn, e-sports players develop expertise as they move through pre-determined game-based scenarios that are often repetitive, but have increasing levels of difficulty. The process of learning is also peer-based and collaborative because participation occurs in pairs or teams, and/or through observations and interactions with peers as spectators via social media. The context of learning is within synchronous and asynchronous online settings and in immersive, virtual and interactive formats. Furthermore, participation occurs in physical and virtual spaces simultaneously, with young people playing together as a school team in the physical classroom against other teams in a virtual environment. In terms of content, e-sports is primarily centred around sport and games.

In digital formats, it is clear that games and sports are highly engaging and inclusive for many young people and, given the exclusive nature of some games and sport provision in formal PE settings (Kirk, 2020), the PE profession might usefully consider e-sports as a companion digital component of the curriculum. Further, the peer-based approach to engagement and participation via spectatorship supports the development of health-related learning outcomes, providing additional challenges to the nature and form of existing PE provision. For instance, participating in e-sports enhances learning in the cognitive and social domains, outcomes which help young people gain the appropriate knowledge, understandings and social skills to be healthy and active throughout their lifetime (Kirk, 2020). Moreover, affective outcomes develop through e-sports participation. Thus, given the few well-established and widely practised pedagogical approaches that influence students' affective outcomes, coupled with reports that teachers have limited skills and resources to facilitate affective learning (Teraoka et al., 2020), e-sports are a potential useful pedagogical tool for teachers to support young people's wellbeing. Controversially, we therefore propose that for some young people, it may be beneficial to incorporate digital PE or even replace elements of traditional PE with digital components in order to positively influence their engagement with physical activity and health.

While the evidence suggests there are clear benefits to e-sports in reaching and engaging diverse groups of young people in sport and games to support physical activity and health outcomes, there are also a number of drawbacks. For example, e-sports is predominantly a sedentary activity and participation in e-sports could further increase sedentary time which may have negative health consequences for young people. It is also worth noting that technologies, like e-sports, have the potential to afford a false sense of autonomy, agency and empowerment (Krutka & Carpenter, 2016). E-sports is a billion dollar enterprise where the design of gaming environments is commercially driven,[12] and educative components and/or the individual learning needs of young people are not prioritised. Hence, the PE profession must approach e-sports with caution and in critically informed ways.

Box 7.2 Case Study Reflective Analysis

Having read the case studies, consider the following questions:

1   How can an understanding of the learning attributes of *#PEwithJOE* and the *British E-sports Championships* be used to encourage the re-design of PE for a digital age?
2   What types of pedagogical experiences should be developed to build on and extend young people's formal and informal health-related learning through digital technologies?
3   How can the design, organisation and delivery of PE be adapted to take advantage of digital affordances?

Training and CPD for PE in a Digital Age

In today's media-rich, technologically innovative environment, schools and teachers are expected to ensure that young people remain healthy and safe online. However, the contemporary digital world differs greatly to the childhood experiences of most teachers which has inevitably created challenges regarding how teachers frame and approach the ways in which they envisage and/or use technologies in PE. Recent evidence also shows that teachers are insufficiently supported to develop their pedagogies to reflect young people's informal learning in a digital age (Goodyear & Armour, 2021; Greenhow et al., 2019). Most initial teacher training programmes and CPD tend to focus on the curriculum and/or how digital technologies can be used to meet pre-determined curriculum outcomes, and there are few examples of evidence-based training programmes that focus on young people's digital behaviours and/or their informal learning through digital technologies (Armour et al., 2017; Casey, Goodyear & Armour, 2016; Greenhow et al., 2019). To better prepare teachers to operate effectively in a digital age, PE teacher training and CPD could usefully shift the primary emphasis from preparing teachers to teach the curriculum to preparing them to work creatively and collaboratively with young people.

Collaborative teaching practices and co-construction will help teachers to develop their digital media knowledge and skills to operate effectively in a digital age. Young people's informal learning through digital mediums is highly dynamic and complex. Thus, to respond in ways that are empathetic to this and pedagogically informed, teachers need to collaborate with their learners in order to understand how PE can be adapted to take advantage of digital affordances for learning. For instance, by collaborating with young people, teachers could develop their knowledge of the learning attributes of young people's informal engagements with technologies. In this regard, the earlier case study reflective analysis could serve as a professional learning resource for teachers to help inform the design of PE, and this could be continually updated and extended as teachers develop new skills. To develop teachers' practices, it might be helpful to refer to some well-established collaborative methods (see Enright & Gard, 2019), and in particular activist approaches (Oliver & Kirk, 2015). Activist approaches are grounded in the involvement and ownership of young people in creating and producing knowledge, where the knowledge produced is used to guide pedagogical decision making and the co-design of learning experiences (Oliver & Kirk, 2015). Through the use of such approaches young people could help adults to better understand the complex and dynamic ways in which they navigate digital technologies and learn how their health is being shaped by technology and, in turn, the types of support that will be relevant for their needs (Oliver & Kirk, 2015).

Co-constructing new knowledge in the local context in real time with young people is particularly important because time lags in policy development and rapid technological change means that much of the external advice that reaches teachers is already outdated (Goodyear & Armour, 2021). At the same time, there is a need for more support from education authorities (e.g. national and governments) and PE professional associations and organisations to ensure that the latest evidence reaches teachers rapidly. The speed at which new technologies emerge and are used and adopted by young people suggests that sporadic training in this area is likely to be woefully inadequate and possibly even harmful. The notion of 'continuous' CPD is also key. Specifically, PE teachers need guaranteed access to the most up-to-date evidence from a range of sub/disciplines, and to be able to deploy a variety of methods, tools and resources to support authentic learning (Armour et al., 2017).

Conclusion

Young people's attitudes towards physical activity and health, and what young people learn, do and understand in relation to health are being continuously shaped by digital technologies. In recognition of this, this chapter has considered the role of PE and the PE teacher and generated new ways of thinking about PE in a digital age. For PE to be effective in supporting lifelong engagement in physical activity, the appropriateness and relevance of PE provision needs to account for young people's learning needs in a digital age. Focussing on learning attributes is one way to structure thinking about a different approach to PE in a digital age. Through such a focus, we explored how contemporary young people learn, how the design, organisation and delivery of PE could be adapted to take advantage of digital affordances, and how initial teacher training and CPD in PE might be changed. While teachers who plan for and enact a new digitally informed approach to PE in the school context will undoubtedly face challenges, it is argued we could better prepare them to operate effectively in a digital age by shifting the emphasis in initial teacher training and CPD from preparing teachers to teach the curriculum to preparing them to work creatively and collaboratively with young people.

Summary and Recommendations

- For PE to be effective in supporting lifelong engagement in physical activity, there is a need to re-design PE to meet young people's learning needs in a digital age.
- One way to structure thinking about a different approach to PE is to focus on learning attributes. Proposed learning attributes for PE in a digital age include emphasis on: personalisation, asynchronous and synchronous learning, peer- and family-based learning and mass (national and global) engagement in learning.
- We need to move beyond simply adding the latest 'gizmos and gadgets' to the current ways in which PE is practised and, instead, rethink how we view contemporary young people and appreciate the holistic and integrated nature of digital technologies in their lives.
- PE teachers need to take advantage of the learning attributes of digital technologies, and use these to: (a) design relevant pedagogical experiences that improve young people's health and wellbeing; and (b) frame the ways in which they design PE policies and practices to enrich young people's informal and health-related learning through digital technologies.
- PE teachers should critically evaluate evidence, enquire into their practices, and develop new insights that are aligned with the needs of their students and their own contexts to meet the contemporary learning needs of young people in a digital age.

Box 7.3 Next Steps

Below are three core activities which we encourage you to complete sequentially to further develop your knowledge about how the design, organisation and delivery of PE could be adapted to take advantage of digital affordances.

1 Identify what types of digital technologies students in your school use and engage with, and evaluate the learning attributes of these mediums.
2 Work with students to co-design learning experiences that enrich their informal learning through digital technologies, and that support them to improve their health and wellbeing.
3 Based on an evaluation of actions 1 and 2, identify the learning attributes for PE in a digital age, and the associated step changes that are required to adapt the curriculum and approaches to initial teacher training.

Notes

1 https://www.thebodycoach.com/blog/pe-with-joe
2 https://www.thebodycoach.com/blog/one-year-of-pe-with-joe-thank-you
3 https://www.bera.ac.uk/blog/pe-with-joe-bloggs-the-rise-and-risks-of-celebrity-teachers
4 https://britishesports.b-cdn.net/wp-content/uploads/2020/09/Champs-Deck-25th-August-v5.pdf
5 https://www.rocketleague.com/
6 https://playoverwatch.com/en-us/
7 https://na.leagueoflegends.com/en-us/
8 https://britishesports.b-cdn.net/wp-content/uploads/2019/07/What-is-esports-PDF-JUL19-V4.pdf
9 https://britishesports.org/news/school-pupils-survey-shows-esports-increases-concentration-behaviour-and-attendance-levels/
10 https://britishesports.org/news/school-pupils-survey-shows-esports-increases-concentration-behaviour-and-attendance-levels/
11 https://britishesports.b-cdn.net/wp-content/uploads/2019/07/AP-Champs-Report-2019.pdf
12 https://britishesports.b-cdn.net/wp-content/uploads/2019/07/What-is-esports-PDF-JUL19-V4.pdf

Bibliography

Goodyear, V.A., & Armour, K.M. (2019). *Young People, Social Media and Health*. London: Routledge.
Harrison, T. (2021). *Thrive*. London: Little Brown Book Group.
Oliver, K.L., & Kirk, D. (2015). *Girls, Gender and Physical Education: An Activist Approach*. London: Routledge.

References

Armour, K.M. (2014). *Pedagogical Cases in Physical Education and Youth Sport*. London: Routledge.
Armour, K., Quennerstedt, M., Chambers, F., & Makopoulou, K. (2017). What is 'effective' CPD for contemporary physical education teachers? A Deweyan framework. *Sport, Education and Society*, 22(7), 799–811.
Casey, A., Goodyear, V.A., & Armour, K.M (2016). *Digital Technologies and Learning in Physical Education: Pedagogical Cases*. London: Routledge.
Chambers, F., & Sandford, R. (2018). Learning to be human in a digital world: A model of values fluency education for physical education. *Sport, Education and Society*, 24(9), 925–938.
Colley, H., Hodkinson, P., & Malcolm, J. (2003). *Informality and Formality in Learning: A Report for the Learning and Skills Research Centre*. London: LSRC.
Ennis, C.D. (2017). *Routledge Handbook of Physical Education Pedagogies*. London: Routledge.
Enright, E., & Gard, M. (2019). Young people, social media, and digital democracy: towards a participatory foundation for health and physical

education's engagement with digital technologies. In V. Goodyear, & K.M. Armour (Eds.), *Young People, Social Media and Health* (pp. 212–224). Oxon, UK: Routledge.

Goodyear, V.A., & Armour, K.M. (2019). *Young People, Social Media and Health*. London: Routledge.

Goodyear, V.A., & Armour, K.M. (2021). Young people's health-related learning through social media: What do teachers need to know? *Teaching and Teacher Education*, 102, 103340. https://doi.org/10.1016/j.tate.2021.103340

Goodyear, V.A., Armour, K.M., & Wood, H. (2018). Young people learning about health: The role of apps and wearable devices. *Learning, Media and Technology*, 44(2), 193–210.

Greenhow, C., Cho, V., Dennen, V., & Fishman, B. (2019). Education and social media: Research directions to guide a growing field. *Teachers College Record*, 121(14), 22.

Greenhow, C., & Lewin, C. (2015). Social media and education: reconceptualizing the boundaries of formal and informal learning. *Learning, Media and Technology*, 41(1), 6–30.

Harris, J., Cale, L., Duncombe, R., & Musson, H. (2016). Young people's knowledge and understanding of health, fitness and physical activity: Issues, divides and dilemmas. *Sport, Education and Society*, 23(5), 407–420.

Harrison, T. (2021). *Thrive*. London: Little Brown Book Group.

Kirk, D. (2020). *Precarity, Critical Pedagogy and Physical Education*. London: Routledge.

Koekoek, J., & Hilvoorde, I. (2018). *Digital Technologies in Physical Education: Global Perspectives*. London: Routledge.

Krutka, D.G., & Carpenter, J.P. (2016). Why social media must have a place in schools. *Kappa Delta Pi Record*, 52(1), 6–10.

Ladwig, M.A., Vazou, S., & Ekkekakis, P. (2018). "My best memory is when i was done with it": PE Memories are associated with adult sedentary behavior. *Translational Journal of the Amercian College of Sports Medicine*, 3(1), 10.

Landi, D. (2017). Toward a queer inclusive physical education. *Physical Education and Sport Pedagogy*, 23(1), 1–15.

Oliver, K.L., & Kirk, D. (2015). *Girls, Gender and Physical Education: An Activist Approach*. London: Routledge.

Powell, D., & Fitzpatrick, K. (2013). 'Getting fit basically just means, like, nonfat': children's lessons in fitness and fatness. *Sport, Education and Society*, 20(4), 463–484.

Quennerstedt, M. (2013). PE on YouTube – Investigating participation in physical education practice. *Physical Education & Sport Pedagogy*, 18(1), 42–59.

Rich, E., Lewis, S., Lupton, D., Miah, A., & Piwek, L. (2020). *Digital Health Generation? Young People's Use of 'Healthy Lifestyle' Technologies*. Bath: University of Bath.

Shapiro, J. (2019). *The New Childhood*. London: Yellow Kite.

Teraoka, E., Jancer Ferreira, H., Kirk, D., & Bardid, F. (2020). Affective learning in physical education: A systematic review. *Journal of Teaching in Physical Education*, 40(3), 460–473.

World Health Organisation. (2020). *WHO Guidelines on Physical Activity and Sedentary Behaviour*. Geneva, Switzerland: World Health Organisation.

8 Physical Education and Health

A Bright Future?

Mike Jess, Paul McMillan and Nicola Carse

Introduction

While PE has been a feature of the school curriculum for more than a hundred years, the subject is still often viewed as sport, games and/or play and has generally had a 'shadowy, marginal existence' in education (Ozoliņš & Stolz, 2013, p. 888). It is therefore not surprising, as highlighted throughout the book (see Chapters 1 and 3), that the teaching of health within PE has been a topic of some debate. This chapter, however, presents a view that the future for PE, and its relationship with health, may be more positive than it has been in the past. Focussing on three related sections, the chapter explores the potential of this new era for PE. First, the 20th century is revisited to create a starting point for the discussion that follows. Specifically, we reflect on the dominant thinking that resulted in the previous century being uncomfortable for PE and for its relationship with health. Building on this, the second section goes on to propose that new and contemporary ways of thinking, supported by physical activity research and widening stakeholder engagement, are creating a new set of conditions to offer a more positive future for PE. In particular, we argue that the shift towards more holistic ways of viewing education, health and PE offers a context in which the subject can develop closer ties with health and take up a more central position in the school curriculum. However, while these new conditions may be encouraging, the disconnection between many of these new developments, alongside the prevailing political conditions, mean that progress is likely to be messy as PE finds itself positioned in a more congested, and possibly contested, context. We conclude the chapter by proposing that three related factors – personal visions, boundary crossing and professional development in context – can help create a framework to bring stakeholders together and support the development of a more educational and coherent PE that is more closely connected to health.

DOI: 10.4324/9781003225904-8

After reading this chapter, you will be able to:

i   recognise how the dominant thinking in the 20th century resulted in a challenging relationship for PE and health;
ii   identify the current conditions that are creating a context in which PE and health can develop a more positive and integrated relationship;
iii reflect on the ways that personal vision, boundary crossing and professional development can help create this more positive relationship between PE and health.

PE Past: A Square Peg in a Round Hole?

As a starting point to inform our discussion, we revisit the 20th century to explore the development of PE and to reflect on its relationship with health (as outlined in Chapter 1). Across the century, two forms of thinking that dominated education in Western cultures had a significant influence on PE and its relationship with health. First, the dominant form of educational thinking, characterised by the privileging of cognitive learning, created a divide between the mind and body, a divide that marginalised the physical. The divisive nature of this mind/body split was exacerbated as traditional modernist practices based on a 'one-size-fits-all' belief increasingly dominated teaching. As such, while the early part of the century saw PE introduced to schooling as a means of improving children's physical health, the dominance of the cognitive domain meant that the subject was positioned on the margins of the curriculum.

In efforts to address this status issue, the second half of the 20th century saw physical educators attempting to align the subject with educational purposes and loosen its links with physical health. Two approaches grappled for dominance during this period: the multi-activity sport approach based on the English public school system (Kirk, 1992), and the more progressive movement education approach (Laban, 1947). Given the nature of educational thinking during this period, the sport-related multi-activity approach aligned with a scientific methodology soon became the dominant curriculum approach, particularly in secondary schools. However, while this approach initially appeared to have some educational merit, its focus on sport techniques (Kirk, 2013) alongside a severe critique of games by leading educational philosophers (e.g. Peters, 1966) resulted in this version of PE still being positioned on the margins of the school curriculum. By the 1970s, many within PE were drawn to the scientific analysis of sport performance as a way for the subject to become included in the cognitively oriented, high stakes national certification systems (Casey & O'Donovan, 2015). Links with health, particularly physical health, became more limited unless they were aligned with fitness regimes and fitness testing in the context of sport (see Chapter 3 for a more detailed scrutiny of this issue). As the century ended, the PE profession was particularly worried about its future role in schools (Hardman & Marshall, 2000).

Emerging Conditions for a Positive Future

As the 21st-century progresses, we are witnessing a shift in the way that many people think about the world, a shift that is having a significant impact on PE and its relationship with health. We suggest that five related conditions are creating a context that is helping to not only integrate PE and health, but also re-position the subject as a more central feature within education (see Figure 8.1).

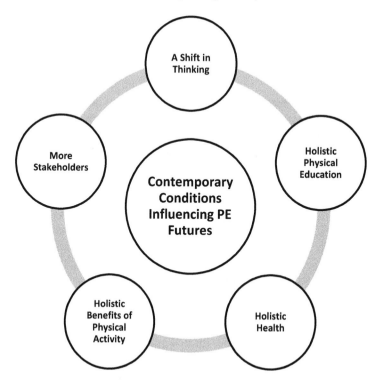

Figure 8.1 Conditions for a Positive Future for PE

A Shift in Thinking

As we all grapple with the complexities of an uncertain world, many academics and professionals now question the traditional types of thinking and practice that have long dominated. There is a clear shift in thinking that sees knowledge and learning increasingly defined in holistic, connected and situated terms (e.g. Biesta, 2015). In a general sense, this shift represents a move towards a more contemporary way of thinking in which learning is 'personal, subjective and unique' (Cohen, Manion & Morrison, 2007, p. 6) and emerges from learning experiences that are more participative and engaging (Davis, Sumara & Luce-Kempler, 2015). Critically, this contemporary way of thinking leads us to acknowledge multiple ways of viewing education, health and PE. We are moving beyond a simple 'one-size-fits-all' approach and are beginning to see different ways of thinking and practising come together because 'it is not possible to tell a single and exclusive story about something that is really complex' (Cilliers, 1998, p. viii). Therefore, while many may remain wedded to traditional practices, contemporary ways of thinking are prompting a significant shift in the way we practise across the education, PE and health sectors.

Holistic PE

As we expand the breadth of our thinking, the impact on PE is seen in the many holistic approaches that have emerged. Holistic approaches offer a more contemporary and connected way of thinking for PE because they not only focus on physical learning but also involve close consideration of the cognitive, social and emotional domains (see Bailey et al., 2009). Examples of these holistic approaches in PE are rapidly appearing on a regular basis and are beginning to change the way many PE curriculum programmes are being taught. Examples include meaningful PE, strengths-based learning, physical literacy, enquiry-based learning, skill theme approaches, student-designed games, non-linear pedagogy, play-based pedagogies, developmentally appropriate practices and models-based practices like sport education and the HbPE Model presented earlier in Chapters 4 and 5.

In addition, there has been a significant increase in PE approaches informed by ecological, socio-ecological and complexity thinking, approaches that focus on developing PE in ways that are more connected and contextually focussed (O'Connor, Alfrey & Payne, 2012; Ovens, Hopper & Butler, 2012; see also Chapter 6). Therefore, while traditional thinking may continue to frame much of what happens in PE, the last 25 years has seen a shift towards a more balanced position in which contemporary educational ideas have gained significant traction in the ways that physical educators think and practise.

Towards Holistic Health Education

In line with these PE developments, there has been a similar shift in health and health education (Glanz, Rimer & Viswanath, 2015). At a theoretical level, this shift is represented by a move beyond the traditional focus on physical disease towards more interdisciplinary and transdisciplinary work. In this vein, holistic, ecological and social ecological perspectives based on the connected and multi-layered nature of health behaviours are now commonly being used to frame developments across health education (see Sallis & Owen, 2015). From a holistic perspective, the integration of cognitive, social, emotional and physical factors increasingly informs developments in health education (e.g. Itharat et al., 2017) and health literacy (Bröder et al., 2017). Indeed, our own Scottish context, similar to Australia and New Zealand (see Chapter 2), has seen the emergence of health and well-being as a core subject area in the Curriculum for Excellence (Scottish Government, 2009) and highlights how this expanding view represents a move towards holistic health.

This shift towards more holistic and ecological thinking in both health and PE, alongside the general shift in thinking across education, represents a significant step forward for PE. Within this new context, and as discussed in Chapter 7, the subject is now aligning with contemporary thinking in education and health education and with the digital spaces that connect to young people's health behaviours. In addition, two further developments offer more encouragement for the future of PE and its relationship with health.

The Holistic Benefits of Physical Activity

In recent decades, research has consistently reported the lifelong benefits of regular physical activity with the result that physical activity has become a prominent feature within policy and practice (see how the PAL project in Chapter 6 strives to reduce the gap between physical activity policies and PE practice). It is particularly encouraging that this research not only focusses on physical benefits but also on a range of holistic benefits linked to developmental, lifestyle, health and well-being factors (see Chapter 2). From a PE perspective, it is important to stress that studies regularly report positive associations between children's physical activity and holistic factors that include 'bone health, muscular strength... self-esteem, anxiety/stress, academic achievement, cognitive functioning, attention/concentration, confidence, and peer friendship' (Chalkley, Milton & Foster, 2015, p. 18). Accordingly, our colleagues Malcolm Thorburn and Shirley Gray at the University of Edinburgh make the point that 'the benefits of increased physical activity for physical, social, emotional and mental wellbeing are contributing to a renaissance in the way physical education related arguments about the education of the body are framed and considered' (2020, p. 1). This more holistic physical activity research subsequently offers strong support for the future of PE and its relationship with health.

More Stakeholders

As PE becomes more visible in education, health and sport, the debate about its future is being played out in a context in which most governments are taking a broader market-driven approach to education and health (Evans, 2014). Politicians, policy makers, national organisations, local authority managers, school leaders, health professionals, sport coaches, voluntary groups, parents/carers, the media and the public are all now more involved in the development of PE. While there may be some drawbacks with this approach (see the next section), the outsourcing of PE sees stakeholders from different sectors now competing for space within this crowded subject area. This situation stops PE remaining a 'closed shop' and expands the range of interested parties who can come together to develop a more coherent and connected educational vision for the subject (Carse, Jess & Keay, 2020).

Potential Barriers

While these five conditions may provide optimism, two potential barriers need to be acknowledged and negotiated if PE is to fulfil its potential and solidify its relationship with health. As contemporary thinking weaves through PE, divisions are unfortunately becoming a regular feature (O'Connor & Jess, 2019). With each new development, PE appears to be fragmenting into different 'camps' as each new group develops its own language and creates specialised interest groups to support specific viewpoints (Tinning, 2015). Davis, Sumara and Luce-Kempler (2015) capture this potential disconnection when, referring to learning theories, they note how each approach is '...like toothbrushes: everyone has one and no one wants to use anyone else's'

(p. 33). Therefore, while the general shift towards contemporary ways of thinking has resulted in many new and mostly welcome developments in PE, there is a concern that the subject area may fragment and lack the common purpose, shared mission and collective identity (Lawson, 2016) needed to develop a coherent and connected subject area.

In addition, while we note a potential benefit from a market-driven approach, this agenda often motivates governments to simplify education by quantifying the relationship between teaching and student achievement. This quantitative agenda sets out to identify the features of 'best practice' that all teachers should implement regardless of social and cultural context (Gale, 2018). This places constraints on teachers' professional judgement and overlooks the adaptive forms of practice required to meet demands across diverse contexts. From a PE and health perspective, this market-driven approach may see a return to the past if too much emphasis is placed on the relationship between PE and physical health. Chapter 3 highlighted how one main driver of fitness testing is often the recording of student progress. With fitness testing practices still prevalent in schools, this could provide a convenient way to further quantify and report student achievement. Therefore, while the conditions discussed earlier may offer encouragement, these two barriers need to be negotiated to enable a positive trajectory for the future.

Moving Forward

In line with the five conditions discussed above, we suggest that three related factors can help physical educators move the holistic educational agenda forward. Together, these factors – personal visions, boundary crossing and professional development in context (see Figure 8.2) – can help to create a framework that will bring stakeholders together and support their quest to develop a more educational, coherent and connected PE.

Personal Visions

As more stakeholders become involved in PE, the 'voice' of physical educators, particularly PE teachers, becomes central to the future positioning of the subject (Jess et al., 2021). Creating this 'voice', however, does not 'just happen' but needs to be actively developed by physical educators as they support each other to describe, enact and share their personal and shared visions for PE: visions that are educational

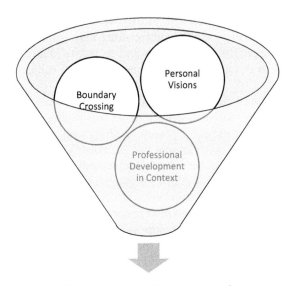

Moving Forward

Figure 8.2 Features to Help PE Move Forwards

and holistic. While PE teachers' work may be rooted in the gymnasium, they also have an important advocacy role across and beyond the school setting. In the classroom, these visions can help teachers recognise the complexities of their students' learning while beyond the classroom they can make a significant contribution to debates about PE and its relationship with education, sport and health. These discussions are likely to be central to the ongoing development of a collective vision for PE and should help teachers build the confidence to share their 'voice' with other educators, professionals, academics and lay-people. Given the current shift in contemporary thinking, the relationship between physical educators and health professionals will have a significant impact on many of these future developments.

At the University of Edinburgh, we have become increasingly aware of the importance of teachers' personal visions for PE. Over the last few years, we have developed 'Visions and Voices', a longitudinal project that seeks to track how teachers develop and share their visions for the subject (Jess et al., 2021). This project now weaves through the four years of our initial teacher education programme and involves the input of 12 university tutors and 400 student teachers (Munro et al., 2022). In addition, university staff are working with early career teachers as they seek to further develop their personal visions in different school contexts. As this project has progressed, we have been encouraged to find that, while the visions of the teachers and student teachers may share key educational, holistic and health-related aspirations, none of these visions are exactly the same and the teachers and students are aware of the need to adapt and even change their visions in different school contexts (McMillan et al., 2021).

Box 8.1 Vision for PE

What is your current vision for PE? In relation to this,

1   How does your vision help focus your practice?
2   In what way(s), and to what extent, does your vision connect with health education?
3   How comfortable are you to share your vision with your PE colleagues and/or colleagues beyond PE?

Boundary Crossing

With calls to move beyond segmented ways of thinking and practising, boundary crossing is becoming a key driver as we move towards more holistic, integrated and ecological approaches in education, health and PE (see O'Connor & Jess, 2019). Questions are regularly raised about individual school subjects being seen as tightly bound specialisms while interdisciplinary and cross disciplinary learning are being extolled as an important way forward. However, if this integrated way of thinking is to become more widespread, the boundaries between subjects will need to become blurred and even broken down to enable more cross disciplinary connection. Critically, because boundary crossing supports more holistic and adaptive ways of working, 'boundary crossers' have a key role to play in turning these interdisciplinary ideas into reality. Thus, boundary crossing will play a major role in the way that physical educators share their visions to develop positive relationships with other stakeholders, particularly those in health.

There are many ways to engage in boundary crossing, but the principles outlined in Box 8.2, adapted from O'Connor and Jess (2019), may be a useful starting point. These principles move beyond traditional, linear approaches by engaging stakeholders in a process that is likely to take time to evolve and develop. The principles acknowledge that boundary crossing involves stakeholders with different starting points so is unlikely to be straightforward and will require some degree of shared agreement to structure the process. For example, discussions about how often and where to meet and how discussions are carried out will probably need to offer some flexibility because consensus may not always be possible, or indeed necessary.

Box 8.2 Boundary Crossing

Reflect on a recent PE and health-related teaching experience. In this scenario, consider the extent to which the following boundary crossing principles were evident.

Principle 1: A Participatory Process with Social and Emotional Consequences
Principle 2: Shared Development of Supportive and Flexible Structures
Principle 3: Taking Time
Principle 4: Acknowledging and Embracing Different Starting Points
Principle 5: Recognising Knowledge is Contested without Need for Consensus

---

Professional Development in Context

Moving professional development beyond the top-down and linear short course mindset that has dominated in recent times is critical for a forward-thinking profession. The inadequacy of this 'sporadic' professional development for PE teachers was highlighted in Chapter 7, in part because of young people's use of rapidly changing technologies to engage with health-related content and physical activity. Therefore, if physical educators are to move beyond a 'quick fix' culture, their professional development needs to be viewed as a long-term learning process that begins during initial teacher education and involves regular revisiting as their careers develop. Critically, this learning process needs to be closely related to their context in class, department, school, community and country. The possibilities for this continuous contextualised learning process are becoming more apparent and we now see approaches such as professional learning communities, action research, practitioner enquiry, self-study, lesson study, peer coaching, learning rounds and collegial visits gradually becoming more popular and available as professional development choices.

This more engaging, collaborative and contextualised process provides opportunities for physical educators to come together and reflect on and adapt their pedagogical practice in a more situated manner. The discussions emerging from this ongoing professional learning create opportunities for physical educators to engage in a boundary crossing process that can help them to adapt their visions for PE over time. Subsequently, professional development of this nature can help physical educators critically reflect on their practice and engage with broader PE and health debates. Indeed, with evidence suggesting that many PE teachers have engaged in little or no health-related professional development, this approach has the potential to address many of the health-related challenges highlighted in Chapter 1.

Box 8.3 Professional Development in Context

Reflecting on your professional development experiences:

1 Consider the extent to which these experiences have been a coherent and connected learning experience and the reasons for this?
2 From a health perspective, what experiences would help you to better integrate PE and health and enhance your PE pedagogies for health in the future?

Conclusion

In this chapter we have argued that, while the relationship between PE and health may have long been debated, the future is likely to become more positive. As the move towards more contemporary ways of thinking continues, holistic and ecological views of knowledge, learning and teaching are becoming a regular feature in education. For PE and its relationship with health, this shift in thinking has created a positive context that is long overdue. With many of the key conditions for a bright future now in place, the next generation of physical educators has the opportunity to become the 'boundary crossers' who can not only create more positive links with health but also a more educational, coherent and connected subject area that sits at the very heart of the school curriculum.

Summary and Recommendations

- The traditional way of thinking in the 20th century not only positioned PE on the margins of the school curriculum but created a challenging relationship between PE and health.
- Today's conditions are creating a positive context for PE to gradually move towards the centre of the curriculum and develop a more productive relationship with health. These contemporary ways of thinking, holistic approaches within education, PE, health and physical activity research, and the active engagement of a wider range of PE stakeholders are all helping to create this positive context for the future.
- Personal vision, boundary crossing and career-long professional development in context are three related factors that have the potential to help frame, develop and enact this positive relationship between PE and health in the future.
- Physical educators are encouraged to engage with these interrelated features to help create a framework that will bring key stakeholders together, develop a more educational, coherent and connected PE, and enact this brighter future for PE and its relationship with health.

References

Bailey, R.P., Armour, K., Kirk, D., Jess, M., Pickup, I., & Sandford, R. (2009). The educational benefits claimed for physical education and school sport: An academic review. *Research Papers in Education*, 24(1), 1–27.

Biesta, G.J.J. (2015). On the two cultures of educational research and how we might move ahead: Reconsidering the ontology axiology and praxeology of education. *European Educational Research Journal*, 14(1), 11–22.

Bröder, J., Okan, O., Bauer, U., et al. (2017). Health literacy in childhood and youth: A systematic review of definitions and models. *BMC Public Health*, 17, 361.

Carse, N., Jess, M., & Keay, J. (2020). Primary physical education in a complex world (part 4): Advocating for the education in primary physical education. *Physical Education Matters*, 15(2), 21–23.

Casey, A., & O'Donovan, T. (2015). Examination physical education: Adhering to pedagogies of the classroom when coming in from the cold. *Physical Education and Sport Pedagogy*, 20(4), 347–365.

Chalkley, A., Milton, K., & Foster, C. (2015). *Change4Life Evidence Review: Rapid Evidence Review on the Effect of Physical Activity Participation among Children Aged 5–11 Years*. London: Public Health England.

Cilliers, P. (1998). *Complexity and Postmodernism*. London: Routledge.

Cohen, L., Manion, L., & Morrison, K.R.B. (2007). *Research Methods in Education*. 6th edn. London: Routledge Falmer.

Davis, B., Sumara, D.J., & Luce-Kempler, R. (2015). *Engaging Minds: Changing Teaching in Complex Times*. 3rd edn. London: Routledge.

Evans, J. (2014). Neoliberalism and the future for a socio-educative physical education. *Physical Education and Sport Pedagogy*, 19(5), 545–558.

Gale, T. (2018). What's not to like about RCTs in education. In: A. Childs & I. Menter, (Eds.), *Mobilising Teacher Researchers – Challenging Educational Inequality* (pp. 207–223). London: Routledge.

Glanz, K., Rimer, B.K., & Viswanath, K.V. (Eds.). (2015). Theory, research, and practice in health behavior. In: K. Glanz, B.K. Rimer, & K.V. Viswanath (Eds.), *Health Behavior: Theory, Research and Practice* (pp. 23–41). San Francisco, CA: Jossey-Bass/Wiley.

Hardman, K., & Marshall, J.J. (2000). *World-wide Survey of the State and Status of School Physical Education, Final Report*. Manchester: University of Manchester.

Itharat, A., Takahashi, T., Sing, R.G., et al. (2017). Holistic approaches for health education and health promotion. *World Heart Journal*, 9(1), 81–96.

Jess, M., McMillan, P., Carse, N., & Munro, K. (2021). The visions and voices of physical education teachers: Part 1. *Physical Education Matters*, 16(2), 51–54.

Kirk, D. (1992). *Defining Physical Education: The Social Construction of a School Subject Post-war Britain*. London: Falmer Press.

Kirk, D. (2013). Educational value and models-based practice in physical education. *Educational Philosophy and Theory*, 45(9), 973–986.

Kirk, D., Macdonald, D., & O'Sullivan, M. (2006). *The Handbook of Physical Education*. London: Sage.

Laban, R. (1947). *Modern Educational Dance*. London: MacDonald and Evans.

Lawson, H. (2016) Stewarding the discipline with cross-boundary leadership. *Quest*, 68(2), 91–115.

McMillan, P., Jess. M., Carse, N., & Munro, K. (2021). The visions and voices of physical education teachers. Part 2: Student teachers. *Physical Education Matters*, 16(3), 52–55.

Munro, K., Jess, M., Craig, M., & McCall, J. (2022). The visions and voices of physical education teachers. Part 3: Weaving vision through initial teacher education. *Physical Education Matters*, 17(1), 71–74.

O'Connor, J., Alfrey, L., & Payne, P. (2012). Beyond games and sports: A socio-ecological approach to physical education. *Sport, Education and Society*, 17(3), 365–380.

O'Connor, J., & Jess, M. (2019). From silos to crossing borders in physical education. *Sport, Education and Society*, 25(4), 409–422.

Ovens, A., Hopper, T., & Butler, J. (Eds). (2012). *Complexity Thinking in Physical Education: Reframing Curriculum, Pedagogy and Research*. London: Routledge.

Ozoliņš, J., & Stolz, S. (2013). The place of physical education and sport in education. *Educational Philosophy and Theory*, 45(9), 887–891.

Peters, R.S. (1966). *Ethics and Education*. London: Allen & Unwin.

Sallis, J.F., & Owen, N. (2015). Ecological models of health behavior. In: K. Glanz, B.K. Rimer, & K.V. Viswanath (Eds.), *Health Behavior: Theory, Research, and Practice* (pp. 43–64). San Francisco, CA: Jossey-Bass/Wiley.

Scottish Government. (2009). *Curriculum for Excellence*. Glasgow: Learning and Teaching Scotland.

Thorburn, M., & Gray, S. (2020). Potentialities in health and physical education: Professional boundaries and change agendas. *Curriculum Journal*, 32(1), 1–13.

Tinning, R. (2015). Commentary on research into learning in physical education: Towards a mature field of knowledge. *Sport, Education and Society*, 20(5), 676–690.

Index

Note: **Bold** page numbers refer to tables; *Italic* page numbers refer to figures and page numbers followed by "n" denote endnotes.

For Product Safety Concerns and Information please contact our EU
representative GPSR@taylorandfrancis.com
Taylor & Francis Verlag GmbH, Kaufingerstraße 24, 80331 München, Germany

www.ingramcontent.com/pod-product-compliance
Ingram Content Group UK Ltd.
Pitfield, Milton Keynes, MK11 3LW, UK
UKHW021423080625
459435UK00011B/133